AGE OF WONDERS

AGE OF WONDERS

Exploring the World of Science Fiction

David Hartwell

Walker and Company  New York

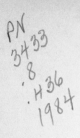

The chapter titled "The Golden Age of Science Fiction is Twelve" originally appeared in slightly different form in *Top of the News* (1982).

First published in the United States of America in 1984 by the Walker Publishing Company, Inc.

Published simultaneously in Canada by John Wiley & Sons Canada, Limited, Rexdale, Ontario.

Library of Congress Cataloging in Publication Data

Hartwell, David G.
  Age of wonders.

  Includes index.
  1. Science fiction—History and criticism. I. Title.
PN3433.8.H36 1984   809.3′876   84-15392
ISBN 0-8027-0808-0

Printed in the United States of America

10 9 8 7 6 5 4 3 2 1

Designed by Laurie McBarnette

DEDICATION

To my parents, Henry G. and Constance N. Hartwell, whose benign support never faltered, in spite of the constant science fiction coming into the house and never leaving

CONTENTS

ACKNOWLEDGMENTS

Many of the ideas incorporated in this book are drawn selectively from the fanzines, reviews, and editorials of the last sixty years, and often from the decades of speeches and panel discussions at SF conventions and late-night personal conversations with most of the names mentioned in the text. Particularly important to the evolution of my thoughts on science fiction have been my continuing discussions with Gardner R. Dozois and Charles N. Brown over the past fifteen years. I wish to acknowledge their special contributions.

Most of all, however, for the past twenty-two years I have been in intense and continuing discussion with Paul Williams about the SF field. It was our joint idea to embody our thoughts on SF in this book, and Paul was present to comment on every page as it came from the typewriter. As special editor and collaborator, this is Paul's book as much as mine. It still surprises us that I was the one to put the words on paper. Thank you, Paul.

AGE OF WONDERS

I

THE SOURCE AND POWER OF SF'S APPEAL

The Golden Age of Science Fiction Is Twelve

Immersed in science fiction. Bathing in it, drowning in it; for the adolescent who leans this way it can be better than sex. More accessible, more compelling. And the outsider can only wonder, What's the matter with him? What is he into, what's the attraction, why is it so intense?

Grown men and women, sixty years old, twenty-five years old, sit around and talk about "the golden age of science fiction," remembering when every story in every magazine was a masterwork of daring, original thought. Some say the golden age was circa 1928; some say 1939; some favor 1953, or 1970. The arguments rage till the small of the morning, and nothing is ever resolved.

Because the real golden age of science fiction is twelve.

THIS is a book about the science fiction field and that body of contemporary writing known as science fiction, or SF. Over the years there have been a number of books on the writing the field has produced, its artwork and illustration, histories, memoirs, even a book devoted to the amateur publications of the fans. But no general attempt to describe both the literature and the specific subculture out of which the literature flows has ever been presented to the world at large. Donald A. Wollheim, in *The Universe Makers,* and Lester del Rey, in *The World of Science Fiction 1926–1976,* come closer than any others and you might try them, though both are dated.

For one thing, the world at large, especially all who do not read and do not wish to read SF, couldn't have cared less. "Everyone" knows that science fiction is not serious literature and that since the word "science" occurs in the name you wouldn't be interested or able to understand if you did try to read it—so why try?

Despite the fact that twelve-year-olds who read it understand it perfectly, and that millions of readers over the years have found it great fun (it *is* supposed to be fun), the majority of educated readers in the English-speaking world spurn SF without reading it or knowing anymore about it than what "everyone" knows. Well, this book is not an attempt to convert anyone (although later on I do recommend some SF for people who have not read in the field before). What I do intend is to offer a book that informs you about an amusing and significant phenomenon that reaches into every home and family in the country and influences the way we all see the world around us.

This is an outsider's guidebook and road map through the world of science fiction, pointing out the historical monuments, backyard follies, highways, and back streets of the SF community—a tour of main events and sideshows, and a running commentary on why the SF world is the way it is. I hope it will be particularly useful for the casually curious, the neophyte reader, and of course the person who knows people in SF and wonders why they are that way. Is your child threatened by this strange stuff, or by the companionship of lovers of science fiction? Does SF rot the mind and ruin the character? Just how wild and crazy are those SF people and what do they really do, where do they come from, why do they stay in the SF world? This tour, if successful, should take you not only through the nooks and crannies of the SF world, but into some unsuspected aspects of the everyday world as well.

Written science fiction, like cooking, mathematics, or rock'n'-roll, is a whole bunch of things that some people can understand or do and some not. We all know people who love cooking, math, or rock (perhaps all three), and others who can hardly boil water, add two plus two, or distinguish music from noise. Your present tour guide stopped trying to convert people to instant appreciation of science fiction years ago when he finally understood that most new readers have to go through a process of SF education and familiarization before they can love it. Just because someone can read does not mean that he necessarily can read SF, just as the ability to write arabic numerals and add and subtract doesn't mean you necessarily can or want to perform long division.

So I have set out to describe science fiction without assuming that you have read any or would even know what to do if you were faced with the text of an SF story. I will discuss as clearly as possible all the barriers you might have against understanding SF and all the barriers that SF has erected to keep from being understood by outsiders—for like the world of the circus and the carny, the SF world only wants insiders behind the scenes. And more, the SF world does not want an audience (such as the "mass audience") who won't take the time to learn the rules and conventions of the game.

SF is special within its community, which has built complex fortifications and groundworks surrounding its treasures; and for most people, the rewards of reading SF or being an SF-type person are worthless or pernicious or even a bit scary. To one who is comfortable and has adjusted to the compromises of our culture, being or becoming something of an outsider has no advantages.

Wait for a moment though, before you make up your mind that you don't really have to become acquainted with what is going on in this other reality. The underground world of SF interpenetrates with your daily world so thoroughly in so many ways that finding out what those relatively few people who live in the SF world are like may let you understand a lot more about how your own world operates. Besides, as Thomas Pynchon so amusingly posited in his eccentric novella, *The Crying of Lot 49,* if you begin to look beneath the surface of everyday life, almost everyone is involved in some sort of underground or underground activity. This kind of activity is so much a part of what everyone does (without ever seeing the big picture) that if you pull back and look at it all, the real world seems very different. That is, in one very real sense, what this book is about.

When you spot a science fiction devotee on a bus, in a library, or on lunch break in the cafeteria, she or he is identifiable only by a display of some kind: She is reading a flashy paperback that says "Science Fiction" on the cover; he is wearing a *"Star Trek* Lives!" T-shirt over his bathing trunks at the beach; she is quietly asking the bookseller if there is a copy of *Women of Wonder* in the store; he is arguing loudly with a friend that *Star Wars* is much better than *Close Encounters* (which is not truly SF) while munching a sandwich and sipping Coke.

Otherwise, there are no reliable outward signs, unless you happen to stop over at a hotel or motel anywhere in the U.S. where one of the at least weekly science fiction conventions is being held—after one look, you switch accommodations, because the whole place is filled with people in costumes, bacchanalian howls, teenagers in capes with swords, normally dressed adults wearing garish name tags that identify them as Gork or Kalinga Joe or Conan or David G. Hartwell or Beardsley Trunion. Your immediate perception of this social situation is either "Feh!" or "Let me back off and view these weirdos from a safe distance, say, at the end of tomorrow's newscast!"

The science fiction person, you see, always lives in the SF world, but under cover of normality most of the time—except while attending a gathering of like minds such as the SF conventions given in understated flashes above. The science fiction reader may be your attorney, your dentist, your children's schoolteacher, the film projectionist at your local theater, your wife or husband or child, happily living in two worlds at once, the real world of science fiction and the dubious reality of everyday life.

If you have lived with or worked with a science fiction person, you will have noticed how intensely she seems to be involved in science fiction, how much she reads it, watches it, recommends to those around her that they try it, because it is her special kind of fun. And if you examine her behavior in everyday life, you may well notice an impatience with the way things are, an ironic, sometimes sarcastic attitude toward everyday things (particularly imposed tasks of a wearisome nature), a desire for change. This complex of attitudes is closely congruent to the complex of attitudes found in the normal human teenager.

In fact, a majority of all science fiction readers are under the age of twenty-one. The question is not how they got that way but why it should surprise anyone that they are. Teenagers are not fully integrated into the tedium of adult life and tend to view such everyday life with healthy suspicion. Quite logical. The science fiction reader preserves this attitude as long in life as his association with science fiction continues, more often these days into full maturity. It makes him act strangely sometimes. But mostly he feeds his head with more science fiction and continues to get the job done, whatever it is.

Nearly a thousand readers of *Locus*, the newspaper of the science fiction field (a semiprofessional monthly published by California fan Charles N. Brown), responded a couple of years ago to a survey, which indicated that the median age of *Locus* readers is twenty-two but that the initial involvement in science fiction of almost every respondent happened between the ages of ten and fourteen. This lends a great deal of substance to the tradition in the science fiction world that active involvement starts early and lasts at least until the early twenties. Science fiction is an addiction (or habit) so reasonable in any teenager who can read (and many who can't very well, in this age of *Star Trek* and *Star Wars*) that it is superficially a curiosity that it doesn't always last. But it doesn't, and most of us do end up well-adjusted, more or less, resigned to life as it is known to be beyond 1984.

The science fiction drug is available everywhere to kids, in superhero comics, on TV, in the movies, in books and magazines. It is impossible to avoid exposure, to avoid the least hint of excitement at Marvel Comics superheroes and *Star Trek* reruns and *Star Wars,* impossible not to become habituated even before kindergarten to the language, clichés, basic concepts of science fiction. Children's culture in the contemporary U.S. is a supersaturated SF environment. By the time a kid can read comic books and attend a movie unaccompanied by an adult, his mind is a fertile environment for the harder stuff. Even the cardboard monsters of TV reruns feed the excitement. The science fiction habit is established early.

In some cases, accompanied by the hosannas of proud parents, a kid focuses his excitement on the science part and goes on to construct winning exhibits in school science fairs, obtain scholarships, and support proud parents in their old age with his honorable gains as a career corporate technologist. Most often, a kid freezes at the gosh-wow TV/comics/movies stage and carries an infatuation with fantastic and absurd adventure into later life. But sometimes, usually by the age of twelve, a kid progresses to reading science fiction in paperback, in magazines, book club editions—wherever he can find it, because written SF offers more concentrated excitement. This is the beginning of addiction; he buys, borrows, even steals all the science fiction he can get his hands on and reads omnivorously for months or even years, sometimes until the end of high school years, sometimes a book or more a day. But the classic symptom is intense immersion in written SF for at least six months around age twelve.

Publishers adore this phenomenon, akin to the addiction to mystery and detective fiction that flourished in the decades prior to the mid-Sixties. One major publisher of SF had been heard to remark that his books are supported by twelve-year-olds of all ages. Every professional writer, editor, and publisher in the science fiction field knows that the structure of science fiction publishing is founded on the large teenage audience, which guarantees a minimally acceptable market for almost every book or magazine published—it requires extreme ignorance and professional incompetence, determination akin to constipating oneself by an act of will, to be unsuccessful when selling science fiction to the omnivorous teenage audience.

What happens to science fiction omnivores? Well, obviously, most of them discover the compulsive excitement of the opposite (or same) sex, and stop reading much of anything for pleasure, most of them permanently. However, once you have been an omnivore, your life has been permanently altered, if only in minor ways. Years later, you may experience an irrational desire to watch *Battlestar Galactica* on TV, even though you know it's dumb stuff. You tend not to forbid your kids or kid your friends if they want a little toke of science fiction from time to time. A news report on solar energy possibilities in the near future doesn't seem like total balderdash, just, perhaps, a bit optimistic in the short run. A front-page newspaper article on the U.S. space probe to Jupiter doesn't read like Sanskrit or form associations with guff like spirit-rapping. Surprise! Your life has been altered and you didn't even notice.

Discovering sex (or competitive sports or evangelical Christianity or demon rum) is not always a total diversion, though. You can, of course, read with one hand. And there are further activities open to the fan in the omnivorous stage: Hundreds, often thousands, of fans gather at conventions every weekend throughout Western civilization (the World Science Fiction Convention of 1979 was in Brighton, England; the 1985 Worldcon will be in Australia) to act strangely together. To a teenage omnivore, such a weekend of license to be maladjusted in the company of and in harmony with the covertly alienated of all ages can be golden. No one much notices how you dress or act as long as you do not injure yourself or others.

Swords and capes (ah! Romance!) are particularly favored among the fat and pimply population, male and female. One wag counted seventy-two Princess Leias at the World SF Convention of 1978 in Phoenix! Star Trek costumes still abound in the mid-Eighties. Or you can hang out in your everyday slacks and jacket or jeans and T-shirt with like minds. And right there among the crowd are all the big-name professionals, from Asimov to Zelazny, by tradition and in fact approachable for conversation and frivolity. Just being there makes you a potentially permanent member of the SF family.

It's a clique, you see. Just like the ones you are cut out of in the local junior high or whatever, only now you are automatically a member until you do something beyond the pale. You might be so shy as to be tongue-tied for your first ten conventions; still, if you walk into a room party you can sit on the floor and listen to Isaac Asimov sing Gilbert and Sullivan—and join in if you like. And go home and tell your friends that you spent time with Asimov last weekend. Just so you don't feel lonely in the arid stretches between conventions you can afford to attend, there are approximately 4,000 fan magazines produced by individuals and written by themselves and/or other fans to keep you in communication with the SF world day to day.

As you might have gathered, the great family aspect of SF is, in the long run, only for the most ardent—maybe 10,000 active fans in the U.S. at any time. Most often, fans mature socially enough to adjust to their home environment and just read the stuff off and on, attending, perhaps, a World Convention every year or two to keep contact with a few friends. This is the chronic stage of addiction, following the active omnivore phase. And *this* stage can last for life.

If you grew up in isolation from movies, TV, and comics and have never read a work of science fiction (or if you tried one once, and found it dumb, incomprehensible or both), you might ask, at this point, why the fuss? The answer is that even if you have kept yourself in pristine separation from the material, you are interacting daily with people who have progressed to at least a stage-one involvement in science fiction and who have altered your environment because of it.

Science fiction as written and published during the last twenty years is so diverse in every aspect that no reader except at the height of the omnivorous stage can expect to be attracted to all of it. And more science fiction has been published in the 1970s and 1980s than ever before: twenty or thirty new paperbacks every month, several magazines, even a number of hardbounds—too much even for the most dedicated omnivore to read. The quality of the individual book or story varies from advanced literary craftsmanship to hack trash, from precise and intellectual visions of the future to ignorant swordsmen hacking their way through to beautiful damsels (less than one-quarter clad) across an absurd environment. There are enough varieties of science fiction and fantasy to confuse anybody.

If you look at a wide spectrum of covers in your local SF paperback section, you begin to notice a lot of categories of science fiction. How do the advanced omnivores and chronics select what to read? By this very process: As in any other kind of book, you can tell the importance of the author of a science fiction book by the size of the author's name on the cover. Another reliable gauge to importance, or at least popularity, is how many copies of an individual title by an author the store has and how many of the author's titles are on the shelf.

But popularity and importance aside, how do you identify whether this is the kind of SF you are looking for? By the complex symbology of the cover. Not always, of course, because the paperback industry (never mind hardcover publishers, who tend to be indeterminate) is guilty of lack of confidence, or ignorance, leading to mispackaging fairly regularly—but in the huge majority of cases, science fiction is quite precisely marketed and packaged.

The images on science fiction covers range from futuristic mechanical devices (which connote a story heavily into SF ideas, or perhaps just science fictional clichés) to covers featuring humans against a futuristic setting, with or without machines (which connote adventure SF) to covers with humans carrying swords or other anachronistic weapons (which connote fantasy or fantastic adventure against a cardboard or clichéd SF background) to hypermuscled males carrying big swords and adorned with clinging hyperzaftig females, both scant-clad against a threateningly monstrous background (which connote sword-&-sorcery or heroic-fantasy adventures, with perhaps some SF elements) to covers representing several varieties of pure fantasy (from rich romantic flowery quests to freaky supernatural horror). Every SF omnivore has sampled all the varieties of SF, from Lovecraftian supernatural horror to the swashbuckling adventure tales of Poul Anderson to the technical and literary conundrums of Samuel R. Delany. Chronic readers usually center their interests in one limited area and read everything packaged to their taste.

The net effect is that there is a rather large number of SF audiences with focused interests, all of which interlock and overlap to form the inchoate SF reading audience. Most individual books reach their targeted audience and prosper from overlap into other related audiences. Occasionally, an SF work satisfies several of these overlapping audiences at once (for example, *Dune* by Frank Herbert) and reaches what the publishing industry calls the mass audience (truly humongous numbers of readers)—and then extends for a decade or more in sales into the audience that consists of normal people who decide to try the stuff and have heard three or four big names (like Robert A. Heinlein's *Stranger in a Strange Land,* which paid most of the light bills in the period 1961 to 1984 for its publisher and allows Mr. and Mrs. Heinlein to visit opera festivals in Europe on whim).

The situation is exceedingly complex. Some say that the whole SF audience (the market) is composed of teenagers, for all practical purposes, and turns over almost completely every three to five years. This theory, the omnivore theory, eliminates all chronic readers from consideration. It has the virtue of practicality from the publishing point of view, though it means you can recycle individual books endlessly and can publish practically anything, no matter how crippled, and reach a basic, dependable, supposedly profitable (though small) audience.

The combined, or omnivore/chronic theory, which is the unarticulated basis behind most SF publishing, would sound something like a classier version of the omnivore theory—keep the good books in print for omnivores who pass into the chronic state and for the non-SF reader who wishes to sample the field through books or authors he has heard of, and scatter the rest of your publishing program among the three spectra (fantasy/ science fantasy/science fiction) in hopes of discovering chronic sellers—works that everyone who reads SF must sooner or later hear about and read. At its best, this philosophy (if we may so dignify a marketing strategy) leads to the publishing of soaring works of the speculative imagination—but mostly it leads to carefully marketed crap. But even that is okay. Both omnivores and chronics are patient and have long memories; they are willing to wade through a fair amount of swamp to find islands of rationality and the real thing—wonderful SF.

It's a kind of quixotic quest, you see, admirable in its way. The SF reader is willing to keep trying, reading through rather large numbers of half-cooked ideas, clichés and cardboard characters and settings in search of the truly original and exciting and good. How many of us outside the SF field could be so determined? The SF reader has fun along the way that is not often visible to outsiders.

The SF reader sneers at fake SF, artificially produced film tie-in novels and stories, most SF films, most TV SF. This he calls sci-fi (or "skiffy")—junk no right-thinking omnivore or chronic should read, watch, or support. But with beatific inconsistency he will pursue his own quest—through endless hours of *Space: 1999, Battlestar Galactica, Mork and Mindy, My Favorite Martian,* and some truly horrendous paperbacks and magazines—in search of something as good as he remembers finding during his initial omnivore excitement. This quest through the rubble is not without its rewards.

Consider: The aforementioned conventions are broken down into discrete areas of programming and many conventions have a general or even quite limited theme. Aside from the World Science Fiction Convention, which is a general gathering of the clans, there is a World Fantasy Convention, numerous Star Trek conventions, a pulp-magazine convention (Pulpcon), Ambercon (devoted to the Amber novels of Roger Zelazny), an SF film convention, numerous "relaxicons" (at which there is no programming—chronics and omnivores gather to party with like minds for a weekend), and literally dozens of localized conventions, ranging from hundreds to thousands of attendees: Pghlange (Pittsburgh); Boskone (Boston); Lunacon (New York City); Westercon (West Coast); V-con (Vancouver); Kubla Khan Klave (Nashville); Philcon (Philadelphia); Balticon (Baltimore); Disclave (Washington, D.C.). The list is extensive, each with a guest of honor, films, panels, speeches, a roomful of booksellers, an art show, and many special events (often including a masquerade), and parties (pretty dependably twenty-four hours a day). Aside from general saturnalia, these conventions build audiences for name authors (guests of honor and other featured guests) and reflect audience fascination with discrete kinds of SF.

The World Science Fiction Convention, a six-day bash, has nearly five twenty-four-hour days of programming. Iguanacon (Worldcon '78), named after a favorite fan animal (Tennessee Williams, *Night of the Iguana:* "Women are fine, Sheep are divine, but the Iguana is el numero uno."), had attendees who came specifically for the Edgar Rice Burroughs Dum-Dum (famed great ape party); feminists and those interested in women writers came for the several Women in Science Fiction events; film fans came for the twenty-four-hour-a-day film programs (a bargain); Georgette Heyer fans came for the Regency Dress Tea (yes, at a science fiction convention); some came to see and hear their favorite big-name authors—heroic fantasy readers to see Fritz Leiber and L. Sprague de Camp, Darkover fans to see Marion Zimmer Bradley, Amber fans to see Roger Zelazny; L-5 fans came to proselytize for space industrial colonies.

Of the almost five thousand attendees, a variety of audiences were represented, often recognizable from the individual package. Aside from the general run of jeaned teenagers and suited publishing types, the Star Trek fans often wore costumes from the show (or at least Spock ears), the regency fans dressed regency, the heroic fantasy fans sported swords and capes, the medieval fans and Society for Creative Anachronism members dressed in a variety of medieval costumes, the women rapped in the special "womenspace" room (the year before there was a "happy gays are here again" party), Princess Leia costumes abounded, and David Gerrold, well-known Star Trek author, handed out David Gerrold fan club cards and buttons. These people filled more than four hotels. Each reader discovers his or her special fun at conventions. Sponsoring similar events, Constellation, the 1984 Worldcon in Baltimore, had about six thousand attendees.

Omnivores tend to form preferences early on in their reading spree, and chronics are usually fixed for life. This is a quick rundown of the main possibilities an omnivore might fix on: classic fantasy (ghost stories, legends, tales); supernatural horror (two categories: classic—from Le Fanu, Blackwood, and Machen to Stephen King and *Rosemary's Baby*; and Lovecraftian, the school of H. P. Lovecraft and his followers); Tolkienesque fantasy (in the manner of *Lord of the Rings*—carefully constructed fantasy worlds as the setting for a heroic quest); heroic fantasy (barely repressed sex fantasy in which a muscular, sword-bearing male beats monsters, magicians, racial inferiors, and effete snobs by brute force, then services every willing woman in sight—and they are all willing); Burroughsian science fantasy (adventure on another planet or thinly rationalized SF setting in which fantasy and anachronism—sword fighting among the stars—are essentials); space opera (the Western in space); hard science fiction (the SF idea is the center of attention, usually involving chemistry or physics or astronomy); soft science fiction (two alternate types: one in which the character is more important than the SF idea; the other focusing on any science other than physics or chemistry); experimental science fiction (stylistically, that is); fine writing science fiction (may include a work from any of the above categories, hard though that may be to accept); single author (reads all published stories of H. P. Lovecraft, his nonfiction, the five volumes of collected letters, the volumes of posthumous collaborations, all pastiches, and so on. Archetypal fan behavior). You can begin to see the enormous variety available.

The most significant development of the last decade for the future of SF is that by about the mid-Sixties, enough "fine writing" had been done in the SF field so that a chronic might fixate on that aspect of SF without running out of reading matter before running out of patience. There has always been excellent writing in the SF field, but now there is an actual audience looking for it—before the Sixties, literate prose was fine when it was found, but was generally irrelevant to the SF omnivores and most chronics.

The increased volume of the fine-writing category has had its effect on outsiders' evaluation of the medium. In the Seventies, the academic appraisal of SF moved from "It's trash" to "It's interesting trash" to "Some of it is important and worth attention, even study." Oh, sigh. Already there are dissertations written by Ph.D.s on science fiction. But SF is alive and still growing, not literary history, and most of the Ph.D. work is a waste of good dissertation paper because many advanced omnivores have read more SF than almost all of the Ph.D.s, and, given the categories presented above, no one has yet been able to define SF well enough so that non-SF readers can figure it out. SF readers know it when they see it, what is real and what is sci-fi (which has come to denote, among the chronics, what is probably admissible as SF but is extremely bad—able to fool some of the people some of the time).

SF people know, for instance, that Superman is real SF. In his book *Seekers of Tomorrow,* Sam Moskowitz tells the story of the teenage fans associated with the creation of the character and its early publication in Action Comics in 1938—and if the first generation of science fiction people had produced nothing more than Superman and Buck Rogers, the effect of science fiction on American culture still would have been profound. Because to the science fiction devotee, SF is naturally carried over into every area of everyday life. She tends to solve problems at work with science fictional solutions or by using the creative methodology learned through reading SF. He tends to see visions of alternative futures that can be influenced by right actions in the present. She tends to be good at extrapolating trends, and especially good at puncturing the inflated predictions of others by pointing out complexities and alternatives. He tends to be optimistic about ecology through technology, has no fear of machines, and tends to be a loner. The science fiction person never agrees with anybody else in conversation just to be friendly. Ideas are too important to be betrayed. Science fiction people, among their own kind, are almost always contentious— after all, a favorite activity is to point to an unlabeled work that may be considered SF and argue about whether or not it is, really, SF.

For the science fiction person, SF is what holds the world together. It is important, exciting, and gives the science fiction person a basis for feeling superior to the rest of humanity, those who don't *know.* The early fans, the generation of the Thirties, many of whom (Forrest J. Ackerman, Bradbury, Asimov, Frederik Pohl, Donald A. Wollheim, and a host of others) are among the major writers, publishers, and editors today, evolved a theory to justify the superiority of science fiction people, then a persecuted, mainly teenage, minority. At the Third Annual World Science Fiction Convention in Denver in 1941, Robert A. Heinlein—then, as now, the most respected author in the field—gave a speech intended to define the science fiction field for its readers and authors. The theme of the speech was change, and it examined the concept and problem of "future shock" nearly thirty years before Alvin Toffler wrote his famous book.

"I think," said Heinlein, "that science fiction, even the corniest of it, even the most outlandish of it, no matter how badly it's written, has a distinct therapeutic value because *all* of it has as its primary postulate that the world does change." He then went on to tell the fascinated audience, in this speech that is legendary even after four decades, that he believed them to be way above average in intelligence and sensitivity—a special group:

> Science fiction fans differ from most of the rest of the race by thinking in terms of racial magnitude—not even centuries but thousands of years. . . . Most human beings, *and those who laugh at us for reading science fiction,* time-bind, make their plans, make their predictions, only within the limits of their immediate personal affairs. . . . In fact, most people, as compared with science fiction fans, have no conception whatsoever of the fact that the culture they live in does change; that it can change.

We can only imagine the impact of such a coherent articulation of alienation and superiority on a bunch of mostly late-adolescent men at the end of the Great Depression. *Though the inferior mass of humanity laughs at us, we are the ones who know, we are the wave of the future, the next evolutionary step in the human race.* If only our pimples would clear up, we could get on with changing the world. Fans *are* Slans! (*Slan,* a novel by A. E. Van Vogt serialized in *Astounding Science Fiction,* about a superior race living in secret among normal humans, was an instant classic in 1941.)

Adults ignore lousy technique when they are being deceived (in literature or elsewhere) if the deception supports the view of reality they have chosen to embrace. Adults stand to lose their sense of security if they don't cling to everyday reality. Teenagers (and the other groups of people described above) have no sense of security as a rule. They are searching for something—change, a future—and unconvincing, mundane reality does not satisfy. Oddly, then, the assumptions made in a science fiction story, which are transparently assumptions and which the young social-reject of any age can share as an intellectual exercise, are more acceptable to him than the everyday assumptions made in a "serious" work of fiction about real (mundane adult) life in which he cannot or does not wish to participate.

Thus the science fiction novel or story is generally aimed at the person who has not embraced a particular set of assumptions about the way things are—this helps to explain both SF's appeal to the young and its seeming shallowness to most "mature" readers. Science fiction is shallow in its presentation of adult human relations (most often the sole concern of most other literature), but it is profound in the opportunities it offers the reader to question his most basic assumptions, even if you have to ignore lousy technique a lot of the time to participate in the illusion. This last is easy for the omnivore and chronic reader—in fact, the minute you overcome the suspension of disbelief problem, admittedly much easier in the early teenage years than in later life, you tend to enter your omnivore stage. Make no mistake—you don't lose your critical ability or literary education when you begin to read science fiction. You just have to learn the trick of putting *all* your preconceptions aside every time you sit down to read. Hah! You were right, this is just another piece of hack work. But the next one, or the story after that may be the real thing, innovative, well written, surprising, exciting.

Throughout the past decade, there has been a growing number of adults who have discovered science fiction as a tool without discovering the thing itself. There are now many new uses for SF in the mundane world: It can be used to combat future shock, to teach religion, political science, physics and astronomy, to promote ecology, to support the U.S. space program, to provide an index to pop cultural attitudes toward science, and to advance academic careers and make profits for publishers, film producers, even toy makers. But the business of science fiction is to provide escape from the mundane world, to get at what is real by denying all of the assumptions that enforce quotidian reality for the duration of the work.

This is reflected in what really goes on at science fiction conventions. Beneath the surface frivolity, cliquishness, costumery, beneath the libertarian or just plain licentious anarchism of the all-night carousing, beyond the author worship, the serious panel discussions, and the family of hail-fellow-fan-well-met, the true core of being a science fiction person is that the convention is abnormal and alienated from daily life. Not just separated in time and space—different! There is no parallel more apt than the underground movements of the last two hundred years in Western civilization: the Romantics in England, Baudelaire and his circle in France, the Modernists, the Beats. (Note to literary historians: This would make an interesting study.) The difference is that to an outsider, it just looks like fun and games, since these people go home after a convention, go back to work, school, housewifery, unemployment, mundane reality, or so it seems.

While they are spending time in the science fiction world, though, things are really different. How different? Let's circle around this for a moment. For instance, you can almost certainly talk to people there who, in normal life, are removed from you by taboos or social barriers. No matter how obnoxious you are, people will talk to you unless you insult them directly, and the chances are excellent that you can find one or more people willing to engage in serious, extended, knowledgeable conversation about some of the things that interest you most, whether it is the stock market or macramé, clothing design or conservative politics, science or literature or rock'n'roll. Science fiction people tend not to be well rounded but rather multiple specialists; the only thing that holds them and the whole SF world together is science fiction. Actually you spend a minority of your time at a convention talking about science fiction, but the reality of science fiction underlies the whole experience and is its basis. For the duration of the science fiction experience, you agree to set aside the assumptions and preconceptions that rule your ordinary behavior and to live free. A science fiction convention, like a work of science fiction, is an escape into an alternate possibility that you can test, when it is over, against mundane reality. Even the bad ones provide this context.

Harlan Ellison, writer and science fiction personality, has spoken of his first encounter with science fiction as a kid in a dentist's office, where he discovered a copy of a science fiction magazine. On the cover, Captain Future was battling Krag the robot for possession of a scantily clad woman; the picture filled his young mind with awe, wonder, and excitement. His life was changed. He wanted more. The reason science fiction creates such chronic addicts as Harlan Ellison is that once you admit the possibility that reality is not as solid and fixed as it used to seem, you feel the need for repeated doses of science fictional reality.

Of course, sometimes what you discover in the science fiction field that attracts you is *not* the thing itself but one of its associates. A chronic reader may actually read almost entirely classical fantasy and Lovecraftian supernatural horror, or a writer such as Fritz Leiber may spend a career writing in every variety of fantasy and science fiction, and yet always be "in the field." There is an interesting investigation to be done someday on why the classical fantasy, a main tradition of Western literature for several millennia, is now part of the science fiction field. In the latter half of the twentieth century, with certain best-selling exceptions, fantasy is produced by writers of science fiction and fantasy, edited by editors of science fiction, illustrated by SF and fantasy artists, read by omnivore fantasy and SF addicts who support the market. Fantasy is not SF but is part of the phenomenon that confronts us.

Since the 1930s, science fiction has been an umbrella under which any kind of estrangement from mundane reality is welcome (though some works, such as the John Norman "Gor" series and the sadomasochistic sex fantasies in a Burroughsian SF setting are admitted but generally despised and generally believed to sell mostly to an audience outside any other SF audience). To present the broad, general context of the SF field, let us consider in more detail the main areas and relationships as they have evolved over the past several decades.

The general question of fantasy has been dealt with frequently, from Freud's well-known essay on the uncanny through recent structuralist works such as Todorov's *The Fantastic,* and is not central to our concern with science fiction. Several things need to be said, however, about fantasy literature before we move on to varieties of science fiction. Fantasy, through its close association with science fiction since the 1920s in America, has developed a complex interaction with science fiction that has changed much of what is written as fantasy today.

H. P. Lovecraft, the greatest writer of supernatural horror of the century, a literary theoretician, and mentor, through correspondence and personal contact, to Frank Belknap Long, Robert E. Howard, Robert Bloch, Fritz Leiber, Clark Ashton Smith, August Derleth, Donald and Howard Wandrei and a number of others, was an agnostic, a rationalist, and a believer in science. His work was published both in *Weird Tales,* the great fantasy magazine between the Twenties and the early Fifties, and in *Astounding Stories,* the great science fiction magazine of its day. Almost all his acolytes followed the same pattern of commercial and literary ties to both areas.

In 1939, after the greatest SF editor of modern times, John W. Campbell, took the helm at *Astounding,* he proceeded to found the second great fantasy magazine, *Unknown,* encouraging all his newly discovered writing talents—Heinlein, Sturgeon, L. Sprague de Camp, L. Ron Hubbard, Anthony Boucher, Alfred Bester, H. L. Gold, Frederic Brown, Eric Frank Russell, as well as Henry Kuttner, Jack Williamson, C. L. Moore, and Fritz Leiber—to create a new kind of fantasy, with modern settings and contemporary atmosphere, as highly rationalized and consistent as the science fiction he wanted them to write for *Astounding.* Through Lovecraft and Campbell a strong link was forged not only commercially but also aesthetically between fantasy and science fiction. Today, and for the last two decades, the most distinguished and consistently brilliant publication in the field has been the *Magazine of Fantasy and Science Fiction,* required reading for all who wish to discover the field at its best and broadest, though it has never been the most popular magazine in the field, always surpassed in circulation by more focused magazines.

After Lovecraft and Campbell, the third towering figure in fantasy so far in the twentieth century is J. R. R. Tolkien, whose *Lord of the Rings* trilogy is both a classic of contemporary literature and an example of the dominant position of the science fiction field as stated above. Tolkien's works, although literary hardcovers at first, were popularized in paperback through SF publishers and have spawned an entire marketing substructure to support works of world-building fantasy in the Tolkien tradition. More books appear every month featuring the quest of a single heroic figure across a detailed and rationalized fantasy world, accompanied by a group of major and minor fantasy characters and ending in a confrontation between Good and Evil, in which Good always wins.

The fourth towering figure is not one person, but is a posthumous collaboration between the artist Frank Frazetta, formerly a comic illustrator, and the author Robert E. Howard, pulp fantasy adventure hack who committed suicide in 1936 the day his mother died and who created a number of fantastic heroes, the best-known of which is Conan the Barbarian. Howard's works had been mostly out of print since his death, except for several small press editions and a few paperbacks, until the early 1960s. Then L. Sprague de Camp obtained the rights from Howard's estate to arrange and anthologize the whole Conan series for the first time in paperback, and to write additions and sequels himself and with others. Through a stroke of genius, comic-strip artist Frazetta was hired to illustrate the paperback covers, which seized the imagination of the audience enough to sell in the millions of copies, established the Howard name, and made Frazetta wealthy and famous. Howard now has nearly fifty books in print in the third decade following his death, and a sword-swinging barbarian hero brutishly adventuring across a fantasy/historic landscape (inside a book with a cover by Frazetta or an imitation) is the principal reading focus of a large number of chronic SF readers. This category, which was formerly called sword-and-sorcery fiction, is now referred to more accurately as heroic fantasy. If Mickey Spillane wrote SF, it would be heroic fantasy. In fact, a hundred years from now SF may have acquired Spillane's works under this rubric.

There are only two areas of fantasy that have not been annexed under the SF umbrella, perhaps because these two areas have never fallen into popular disrepute: Arthurian romances and the occult horror best-seller. There are indications that these two areas may remain separate and independent—both types tend to be written by authors who have no desire to associate themselves and their works with low-class, nonliterary, low-paying (until recently) stuff.

The only science in all the areas of fantasy is either straw-man science (which cannot cope) or black science (used by the evil sorcerer). Amoral science is a recent addition to some heroic fantasy (especially noticeable in the works of Michael Moorcock), as is the idea of magic as a scientific discipline (a contribution of the Campbell era). And I can generalize without fear of contradiction by saying that except in a tiny minority of cases, technology is associated with evil in fantasy literature. So it is particularly curious that the element of estrangement from everyday reality has come to yoke by itself the two separates, fantasy and science fiction, even though SF was invented to exclude "mere" fantasy. This complex of seeming contradiction will be investigated in more depth shortly. For the moment we will move on to a consideration of the subdivisions of the center of the field, science fiction.

Hugo Gernsback, who invented modern science fiction in April 1926, knew what he meant by "scientifiction" (as he named it) and assumed it would be evident to others: all that work Wells and Verne and Poe wrote ("charming romance intermingled with scientific fact and prophetic vision," as Gernsback says in the editorial in the first issue of the first magazine, *Amazing Stories*). In addition to this confusion, Gernsback, an eccentric immigrant and technological visionary, was tone deaf to the English language, printing barely literate stories about new inventions and the promise of a wondrous technological future cheek by jowl with H. G. Wells, Poe, Edgar Rice Burroughs (!), and a growing number of professional pulp writers who wanted to break into the new market. The new thing was amorphous, formed and re-formed over the decades by major editors and writers, and all the chronic readers, into the diversity that is science fiction today.

It is a source of both amusement and frustration to SF people that public consciousness of science fiction has almost never penetrated beyond the first decade of the field's development. Sure, *Star Wars* is wonderful, but in precisely the same way and at the same level of consciousness and sophistication that SF from the late Twenties and early Thirties was: fast, almost plotless stories of zipping through the ether in spaceships, meeting aliens, using futuristic devices, and fighting the bad guys (and winning).

By now it should be obvious that we are dealing not with a limited thing but with a whole reality. More than an alternate literary form or an alternate life-style, science fiction is coequal reality, informing the lives of thousands and affecting the lives of millions, a fact of life more intimate than inflation, whose influence is so all-pervasive that it is traceable daily in every home, through the artifacts and ideas that represent all possible futures and all possible change.

2 "I Have a Cosmic Mind—Now What Do I Do?"

The science fiction world orbits around the fictions, the stories and the ideas in them, and the writers who produce the works. What is *in* science fiction that binds readers to it? Much of my continuing examination here and in the following chapters will be devoted to the attractions SF exerts on readers and writers and how these attractions distinguish SF from other varieties of contemporary literature.

Science fiction has flowered and prospered in our troubled and fast-evolving century in part because it alone among contemporary literatures consistently deals with the big questions: What are we here for? Where are we going? How much worse can things get? Modern readers, especially the young, no longer believe in or even necessarily desire a stable universe. And as a kind of defense, they have learned to find pleasure in studying the big picture: the long view of human history and human affairs apparent in the SF enterprise. There is a fascination in kicking around ideas when you know that ideas can and will alter objective reality.

ABSTRACT ideas are made flesh through science fiction. Except for all these crazy stories about space and time, radically distanced from the mundane, the literature of ideas is pretty much moribund in the latter half of this century. Popular magazine articles, scholarly essays, speculative nonfiction such as all those Bermuda Triangle books, flying saucer stuff, is mostly degraded and disenchanting. Hardly enough, as they say, to keep the mind alive. And badly written to boot. About the only writing other than science fiction in the last decade in which you can find complex and wonderful speculation is in certain scientific and technical journals, with their quarks and quasars, black holes and drifting continents. But the context of these journals makes them inaccessible to all but a few specialists (a few of whom—eureka!—are science fiction writers, friends of science fiction writers, or fans).

And that's not all. Numerous science fiction writers are omnivorous readers, their knowledge an enormous kitchen sink of ideas and speculations from ten or a hundred different disciplines. A new theory in any field (history, economics, biology, home ecology, gestalt psychology) gets transformed very quickly by someone, somewhere, into a science fiction story. It all started with Poe and Verne, who developed an aesthetic of using knowledge, especially contemporary scientific knowledge, as a literary device to achieve or increase verisimilitude. Verne, especially, was interested not only in theory but also in speculative technology, so he read widely in natural science journals and presented wonderful devices, such as high-tech balloons, submarines, and airplanes, which he found in those journals.

James Blish was fascinated by Toynbee's cyclical theory of history, so he wrote his great four-volume series, *Cities in Flight,* to demonstrate his version of how this theory would operate in a galaxy-wide civilization over enormous time spans. Robert A. Heinlein combined a whole complex of economic, political, semantic, and technological ideas into a huge chart, a history of the future, which he used in the early 1940s to write the stories and novels in his masterful Future History series. A. E. Van Vogt in the early Forties developed a theory of science fiction writing which dictated that a story or novel should be

written in approximately 700-word blocks, with a new speculative idea introduced in every block (a dizzying aesthetic that no
one but Van Vogt ever practiced). And if a writer hasn't got any
firsthand ideas, then secondhand ideas are perfectly acceptable,
as long as she or he handles them in a new and exciting
manner.

Of course science fiction is not all big ideas, and some of the
best SF is really about very old ideas (age-old religious controversies, the whole range of the histories of philosophy and
society). The science fictional histories of the future are rife
with monarchies, feudal estates writ large, democracies, oppressive dictatorships—not generally very innovative. But the best
SF always deals with ideas, as opposed to fantasy, which almost
always deals with morality, ethics, and the inner life of characters.

What happens when a science fiction writer gets excited by a
big idea? Well, when any idea begins to irritate the consciousness, you begin to play with it, turn it every which way, see if
the reverse is true (or interesting), begin to feel the onset of
thematic insight, a flash of meaning or possible meanings. Jim
Gunn tells the anecdote about reading an encyclopedia article
on pleasure, which ended with the stylish grace line "but the
real science of pleasure has not yet been invented." He was
stopped in his tracks and immediately began to think about a
possible science of pleasure, what it would entail, and then
wrote his novel *The Joymakers,* about a future world ruled by
the science of hedonics.

Ideas are everywhere, but there are no big ideas unless they
grow in the mind of the writer into something that allows the
world to change utterly, to change in a manner that has the
broadest thematic implications. What if humanity could actually attain the eternal frontiers of space and time, if whole
universes of alternate possibilities really exist, if time began to
run backward, if part or all of humanity were immortal, if
humans could attain through evolution or technology a whole
spectrum of mental powers, if there are truly alien intelli-
gences, if any of a thousand speculations can be posited as true?
What kind of exciting, frightening, wonderful, depressing times
might human characters be living through if any of these big

things happened, how, precisely, might they happen, and how would things work?

Ursula K. Le Guin addresses this point in her trim little essay, "On Theme" (in *Those Who Can,* ed. Robin Scott Wilson, New York: Signet, 1973, pp. 204–205):

> Every now and then one can say of a specific short story that it did begin with a single, specific idea, with a single, specific source. This is the case with "Nine Lives."
>
> I had been reading *The Biological Time Bomb* by Gordon Rattray Taylor, a splendid book for biological ignoramuses, and had been intrigued by his chapter on the cloning process. I knew a little about cloning . . . but so little that I had not got past carrots, where it all started, to speculate about the notion of duplicating entire higher organisms, such as frogs, donkeys, or people. I did not have to read between the lines: Rattray Taylor did it for me. He pointed out that some biologists have been contemplating these more ambitious possibilities quite seriously (why don't people ever ask biologists where *they* get their ideas from?). In thinking about this possibility, I found it alarming. In wondering why I found it alarming, I began to see that the duplication of anything complex enough to have personality would involve the whole issue of what personality is—the question of individuality, of identity, of selfhood. Now that question is a hammer that rings the great bells of Love and Death. . . .
>
> I don't think SF writers merely play with scientific or other ideas, merely speculate or extrapolate; I think—if they're doing their job—they get very involved with them. They take them personally, which is precisely what scientists must forbid themselves to do. They try to hook them in with the rest of existence.

And that is a distillation of what happens when things go well.

Of course a high percentage of the time, the SF writer is off base, sometimes even way out in left field, either in regard to scientific probabilities or to human nature and thematic implications—and sometimes the obvious purpose is to provide rip-roaring adventure against a science fictional background. Still, the distance between mundane reality and the reality of the given SF story gives a size and scope to SF—authentic or illusory as the case may be—that's big, wonderful, mind-stretching. You can find things you never thought of, or thought possible, or thought of in that way, in every SF story.

In Kurt Vonnegut's *God Bless You, Mr. Rosewater* (New York: Dell, 1965, p. 27), Eliot Rosewater, an inveterate reader of SF, drunkenly addresses the Milford SF writers conference—an actual event, which Vonnegut once attended:

> I love you sons of bitches. . . . You're all I read anymore. . . .
> You're the only ones with guts enough to *really* care about the
> future, who *really* notice what machines do to us, what wars do
> to us, what cities do to us, what big, simple ideas do to us, what
> tremendous misunderstandings, mistakes, accidents and catas-
> trophes do to us. You're the only ones zany enough to agonize
> over time and distances without limit, over mysteries that will
> never die, over the fact that we are right now determining
> whether the space voyage for the next billion years or so is going
> to be Heaven or Hell.

Prophets without honor, that's how Eliot sees the SF writing community of nearly twenty years ago. And Eliot, we can see, lives in the SF field we have been talking about, is part of the family, especially since he lives in a real world that he cannot communicate to the other inhabitants of mundane reality, a world of big ideas. Eliot with all his heart wants to act out some of those big ideas and to the extent that he does, he gets himself into a heap of trouble.

Someday some good literary scholar will do an illuminating comparison between Eliot and Jack Isidore, of Seville, Ca., the central character of Philip K. Dick's *Confessions of a Crap Artist.* Jack is a creep and a weirdo but is essentially kind and humane, caught in the grip of one big idea after another—he's a science fiction fan, among other pursuits. He's never quite able to tell the good ideas from the bad, having none of what we usually call common sense, until he's lived with them for a while. Meanwhile, all the supposedly saner people around him, who consider him a harmless nut, boring and bothersome, are being cruel to one another, acting out selfish and petty fantasies and believing themselves superior to Jack.

Eliot Rosewater and Jack Isidore, however, have nothing on Claude Degler, superfan and founder of the Cosmic Circle.

Degler attended the Denver convention as a young fan. His travels around the SF family make fascinating reading; they are chronicled in Harry Warner's history of the doings of early SF enthusiasts up to about 1950, *All Our Yesterdays*. First Degler created a hotbed of SF fan activity, clubs full of local SF enthusiasts in and around the town of New Castle, Indiana. Then, in 1943, the Cosmic Circle went nationwide, "so that cosmic fandom will actually be some sort of power or influence in the postwar world of the near future." The members of the Cosmic Circle began to deluge SF fans everywhere with material on the group, all, according to Harry Warner, "containing symptoms of deriving from the same mind, typewriter and mimeograph" (p. 189):

> Declaration of existence: of a new race or group of cosmic-thinking people, a new way of life, a cosmology of all things. Cosmen, the cosmic men, will appear. We believe that we are actual mutations of the species.

Such was the opening manifesto of the Cosmic Circle. Fans of the era were either horrified or just amused, depending on their paranoia quotient. Jack Speer, a well-known fan at the time, arranged through friends to send Degler a series of postcards from around the country, all inscribed, "I have a cosmic mind—now what do I do?"

Degler's enthusiasm created a microcosmic scandal, a bizarrely energetic effort to unite the fan world into an elitist movement. What Degler had done was to assemble all the half-serious, juvenile, and utopian self-aggrandizers among differing groups within the SF family, put them together, and assert their literal truth. The Cosmic Circle was in essence a call for support for all these assertions so that the SF family could be important in the real world of the future. But everyone with any common sense in the SF world knew that most of this stuff just wasn't true.

Claude Degler was verifiably last seen on the West Coast in 1950—he borrowed fifty cents from a fan in San Francisco for transportation—though recently he is supposed to have appeared at a small convention in the Midwest. Or perhaps not. The net effect of Degler on the SF field was, in the end, to create an historic controversy that only confirmed the essential premises of "agreement to disagree," a basis of unity in the SF world. Fans and writers may propose any kind of idea, big or small, for consideration and discussion (for which read disagreement). But the idea must be distanced in some way from the mundane world so that it can be thought about and discussed—but not necessarily acted upon. Going out and trying to put big ideas into practice, like Jack Isidore or Claude Degler or Eliot Rosewater did, can get you crucified, after all.

But the big ideas of science fiction do interact with the real world, though not usually in a direct cause-and-effect manner. Let us consider the most popular SF of the last couple of decades.

Dune, by Frank Herbert, is one of the two most popular science fiction novels of the last twenty years; the other is Robert A. Heinlein's *Stranger in a Strange Land. Dune* is an epic romance about ecological/political/economic struggles in a galactic empire in the far future. Its hero, Paul Atreides (the name invokes a whole structure of Greek tragedy), is considerably larger than life, the culmination of a thousand years of secret genetic manipulation and the product of the toughest formal and informal training any young prince ever went through. Happily for the effectiveness of the novel, we go through this training and experience with the hero: The tone of the book is instructive, which is flattering, not annoying, since who among us doesn't want to learn how to be Prince of the Universe?

The strengths of the book are setting, plot, characterization, and suspenseful writing (in the clear, precise, naturalistic mode). The characterization is mainly in terms of good and evil, strength and weakness, and is completely effective in spite of a lack of full rounding and depth. The plot is complex but not episodic; everything that happens is necessary to the story and follows logically from the original premise: the exile of the Atreides family to the desert planet Dune. The setting of *Dune* is its special achievement: The story depends completely on the interaction of the hero with the setting, the ecosystem of Dune.

Briefly, the Atreides family is locked in a deadly power feud with the Harkonnen family, and shortly after Paul and his parents arrive on Dune the Baron Harkonnen succeeds in having Paul's father, Duke Leto, murdered. Paul and his mother escape into the desert that covers most of the surface of the planet; there they meet the Fremen, the tough, nomadic natives of Dune. Here the importance of the setting begins to be emphasized: The Fremen have so little water that they wear suits that conserve every milliliter of sweat, urine, and exhaled vapor; when a person dies, they drain the water from him. The toughness of their environment has made the Fremen geniuses at survival and forced them to become a very tight, sometimes brutally efficient, tribal unit. Fremen training and consciousness give Paul the edge he needs to survive and triumph in the cosmopolitical struggles ahead.

On Dune the key factor in both economics and ecology is the addictive spice, *melange*. This is the planet's greatest natural resource for interplanetary trade (Herbert foresaw in *Dune* the Arab role in our current energy crisis—after all, his first novel, *Under Pressure*, written a decade before *Dune*, was about future oil thievery among nations). The spice also turns out to play a critical part in the complex ecological process that keeps Dune from running out of water altogether. And its hallucinogenic properties arouse Paul's latent prescience, giving him mystic moments of painful knowledge of the future. And more.

All these elements of the story merge perfectly into climactic resonance and resolution, which is not so much the triumphant battle against the Harkonnens as the implied triumph-to-come from the Fremen effort to turn their desert planet into a paradise—a triumph not of technology but of ecological planning and awareness.

Dune was published in 1965. By 1967 it was already a cult book; a mention of the word "ecology" in a college dining hall or in the office of an underground newspaper would immediately bring the response, "Have you read *Dune?*" It is quite possible that the emergence of ecology as a popular idea in the mass media in the late Sixties and early Seventies can be traced to the impact of this one science fiction novel on youthful opinion-shapers. The word "ecology" is prominent in *Dune*. Even for the reader who'd heard the word before, *Dune* was an effective introduction to its powerful implications, and the book is still one of the only novels in any genre that makes constructive awareness of one's place in his ecosystem a heroic quality. Most of the other works of fiction that deal with the theme at all are just eco-disaster novels.

In looking for the reasons for *Dune*'s popularity, we have to note that it is an unusually well-drawn and effective adventure story on a grand scale, and is at the same time something more: a book with immediate and intentional relevance, a moral allegory of our own time that can be grasped immediately as such, even by the very young.

Dune's success over the years has been enormous and significant. It has sold millions of copies in numerous editions, and when Herbert completed the third book of the *Dune* series, *Children of Dune*, it became an authentic hardcover best-seller with 75,000 copies sold (not including book club sales). It was the first hardcover best-seller ever in the science fiction field, by a science fiction author, with a science fiction cover, with science fiction written all over it. *Children of Dune* proved to the publishing industry that science fiction could make it big without denying the name. And *Dune* itself continues to sell at a wonderful rate in the 1980s—it may be the best-selling SF book of all time. It would be pointless to deny the potential effects of such a book with such a record. *Dune* is a book that entertains and educates.

Star Trek is a phenomenon rather than a book, but in a discussion of how SF deals with big ideas and how those ideas begin to impinge more or less directly and immediately on our daily lives, *Star Trek* is as significant an example as *Dune*. *Star Trek*, however, does not deal with ideas in the tradition of written SF. Originally a TV show that was canceled in spite of a heroic letter-writing campaign by its committed fans, the *Star Trek* world refused to stay canceled. It has become apparent that *Star Trek* is about ideals and idealism in a science fiction setting, ideals which are not discussed but rather embodied and projected.

Star Trek fiction offers a kind of *Reader's Digest* approach to science fiction—snappy, compact summaries of standard SF plots and clichés. The familiar flat characters and cardboard starship serve to make SF ideas accessible, and therefore excit-ing, to an audience familiar otherwise only with "sci-fi." It's an undemanding audience that reads very little prose that makes demands on it, basically style-deaf.

However, the execution of the *Star Trek* books and show does not detract from the essential emotional appeal of *Star Trek*. The starship *Enterprise* and its crew represent an ideal civiliza-tion, a utopian community in which all races and types of humanity live in harmony according to the highest (1960s American) ideals. The characters are all representative types, both professionally and racially, under the benevolent com-mand of Captain Kirk. External problems constantly invade this perfect society; these problems are solved neither by force nor technological knowhow but by emotional adjustment. Each story has this emotional dimension, in which the stability of the perfect society is challenged and one of the central characters must respond, with humane emotion as well as logic, to restore harmony.

Mister Spock, the half-human Vulcan who is racially incapa-ble of showing emotion, is a pivotal character, a constant embodiment of the war between logic and feeling, himself a challenge to the emotional stability of the *Enterprise.* He is a symbol of repressed emotion (bad) who constantly implies emotional virtues (good) in his loyalty to Kirk and to the crew of the ship. Thus is the godless power of science tamed by future society.

The *Enterprise* is an idealized future of humanity, the heaven of many science fiction readers. Each episode of *Star Trek* starts and ends at home in utopia. The archetypal cry of the *Enter-prise* crew after any adventure is, "Beam us home."

All of which is very comforting to the readers. It reinforces unsophisticated idealism, offers an optimistic picture of the future, and provides the reader an orderly world of romance and adventure to escape to when the "real" world is oppressive or boring.

The first *Star Trek* books filled twelve paperback volumes of short stories by James Blish, a veteran science fiction writer who applied none of his varied talents to the task but instead tried to reproduce the effect of the original TV episodes as accurately as possible. There followed several volumes of stories from the animated *Star Trek* Saturday morning TV series, then novels by various hands featuring the world and characters, billed by the publisher as "new *Star Trek* experiences." And every year throughout the Seventies more and more nonfiction and associational books appeared. With the advent of the 1980s, and *Star Trek: The Motion Picture,* a whole spate of new books and films have appeared, proving the continuing vitality of the *Star Trek* world, in which ideals are right up front and important.

Furthermore, as the Seventies progressed, Gene Roddenberry (the creator of *Star Trek*) and the original stars of the series began to be interested in the U.S. space program, to speak in public in favor of NASA's efforts. Nichelle Nichols (Lieutenant Uhura) actively toured and recruited for NASA. All this culminated in a huge letter-writing campaign among *Star Trek* fans, which succeeded in convincing President Ford to name the first actual space shuttle the *Enterprise.* Perhaps it is still too early to assess the impact of *Star Trek* on two decades of American children, but there are a whole lot of young supporters of space exploration in the U.S. today.

Not many older SF people have participated in the *Star Trek* phenomenon, but the feelings of the SF community as a whole toward *Star Trek* have been generally benign, especially since the *Star Trek* fans began to hold their own conventions in the early Seventies and stop (for the most part) demanding time for *Star Trek* events at the regular round of SF conventions. Addiction to *Star Trek* has been known to lead to omnivorous reading of science fiction, so the regular SF chronic suffers *Star Trek* as a slight embarrassment that probably does more good than harm.

However (until it became unfashionable in some circles in the recent past), like Trekkies, the whole science fiction field has always supported space travel in the real world. In the earliest days of science fiction, in the late Twenties and early Thirties, science fiction readers were often out on weekends building small rockets; were in correspondence with German experimenters such as Willy Ley; and were uniformly optimistic about space and space travel. The first place Wernher Von

Braun came when he reached New York was to a local science fiction convention. And the great names of modern science fiction, Isaac Asimov, Arthur C. Clarke, Ray Bradbury, and Robert A. Heinlein, at one time or another appeared in public in support of the U.S. space program, and of course have promoted it through their fiction.

Space travel was *the* big idea of science fiction right up through the 1950s. It is not an overstatement to say that the whole SF field believed that the future of humanity lay, immediately or ultimately, in space. SF magazines such as *Space Science Fiction Magazine, Rocket Stories, Space Stories, Wonders of the Spaceways,* and a number of others evidence this focus. Writers and readers believed in space travel. They wanted that future full of adventure among the planets and stars to be real.

In 1947, after his service in World War II, Robert A. Heinlein moved from Philadelphia to Hollywood. He was already the embodiment of the best in science fiction, already possibly the most popular SF writer in the world. And he moved to Hollywood with the announced intention of writing the first real American SF movie, about the first flight to the moon. He succeeded. *Destination Moon,* technologically accurate and based on Heinlein's script, was the film that started the great cycle of science fiction films in England and America in the 1950s. At the same time, Heinlein was writing his famous novella, "The Man Who Sold the Moon," about D. D. Harriman, a visionary industrialist who causes the first rocket to the moon to be built. This was the glowing bright side of SF in the years when the other big idea of prewar SF that John W. Campbell had promoted—the power of the atom—had turned frightening. Nothing could stop Heinlein, then or now.

Robert A. Heinlein, the dean of science fiction writers, has written thirty-eight books, all science fiction, with total sales of over thirty million copies. His position as the leading SF author has been firmly established since the early 1940s. Heinlein always gives us a darn good yarn (as he would say) peopled by attractive characters and their amusing, instructive conversations, and full of fascinating, smoothly tossed-off details of the future.

Heinlein's books fall roughly into three categories: his recent novels (1959 to date); his earlier works, including both novels and short stories (1939–59); and his "juveniles," twelve novels written between 1947 and 1959 expressly for the teenage market, many of which, however, were initially serialized in adult SF magazines. By the same token, Heinlein's "adult" books are read by young people as enthusiastically and indiscriminately as his juveniles are read by adults.

Heinlein's early novels and stories usually hypothesize a future situation—What would happen if the U.S. turned into a religious autocracy (*If This Goes On*)? What would happen if society discovered a group of people in our midst who have secretly used genetics to achieve an average life-span twice as long as the rest of us enjoy (*Methuselah's Children*)? What would happen if the leader of a world government were replaced by an actor impersonating him (*Double Star*)?—and then develop this situation to its logical conclusion. His stories have charm and depth; they can be read and reread with constant pleasure.

The Heinlein juveniles differ from his early books mainly in having a young adult protagonist, usually but not always male. They are less self-conscious than the adult books about offering instruction, mostly in astronomy and survival. Heinlein often includes as a major character a lovable and intriguing alien who becomes pals with the protagonist—this same prototype shows up in several of his later works as an intelligent computer. The books are upbeat in tone; the protagonists have interesting rough times, go through a maturing process, and end up with bright futures.

One thing the juveniles and much of Heinlein's early work have in common is a real enthusiasm for space travel, a sense of wonder about exploring the solar system and eventually leaping into interstellar space, and a reverence for scientifically and technically accurate detail about space travel.

Precisely at that moment in the late 1950s when space travel became a reality, shocking most of the world, Heinlein's interests and his fiction turned in other directions. In 1961 he published *Stranger in a Strange Land,* his most famous and controversial novel, a full-scale satire on the taboos of Western civilization. If H. G. Wells and Rudyard Kipling are the paradigms of early Heinlein, then perhaps George Bernard Shaw—garrulous, long-winded, brilliant and satirical, especially the Shaw of *Back to Methuselah*—is the paradigm of Heinlein in *Stranger* and after. For *Stranger* is for the most part a series of dialogues in a dramatic SF setting through which ideas are discussed: set pieces on art, cannibalism, sex, religion, and a myriad other topics, attacking cultural prejudice with logic. (Logic always wins.) *Stranger* is principally about religion, but within its framework Heinlein creates perhaps the most universal of all SF novels about ideas.

Stranger was unquestionably the most popular SF novel of the 1960s, selling millions of copies and becoming, for good or bad, the great cult book of the hippie movement. Heinlein's logical attack on American culture and the social shams that limit personal freedom was consistent and deadly, just exactly what a generation of youngsters disillusioned by the fall of Kennedy's Camelot, the rise of the war in Southeast Asia, and the failure of peaceful demonstrations against racism needed to express their own frustration and then point out paths elsewhere. *Stranger* became a sacred text. A number of people even attempted to put the religion of *Stranger* into practice, including Charles Manson, whose selective interpretation of the practices of Valentine Michael Smith, one of the central characters, permitted Manson to "discorporate" evildoers in the name of right and justice. Poor Heinlein. Poor us.

Heinlein's examination of social, economic, political, and cultural ideas has continued throughout his later works, his method has remained the same and his sales have not flagged. But with *Stranger* he turned away from the wonders of science and technology as a wellspring of ideas, the kinds of ideas for which SF is known and by which it is characterized in the public mind.

The big visionary technological idea has been the hallmark of Arthur C. Clarke's great career in SF. His first big success was *The Exploration of Space,* a nonfiction best-seller in 1950. But it was the success of *2001: A Space Odyssey* in 1968 that finally catapulted him into wider public recognition, a success attributable to the sense of wonder the film projects through its loving attention to technological detail and its awesome, mystical thematic content.

Arthur C. Clarke is an example of the excellent science fiction writer who probably couldn't succeed in any field of writing other than SF or popular science. His great assets are his knowledge of and enthusiasm for the details of astronomy, astrophysics, and oceanography, and his prodigious visual imagination when applied to the experiences humans may have in their exploration of space and the ocean depths. Clarke's other talents—his ability to plot (which is good) and to characterize (rather poor)—don't add up to much when you take away his enthusiasm for describing science fictional environments. His popularity in SF stems from the fact that, for all his interest in science (indeed, as a result of that interest), he is a romantic and a mystic, and even more than Heinlein he succeeds in making space travel an authentically romantic experience.

"The Sentinel," a Clarke story written in 1952 that was the inspiration for *2001,* gives us a portrait of a romantic scientist (he likes to look at moonscapes and climb lunar mountains) who has a rational, tangible, yet mystical experience. He discovers a pyramid surrounded by a force field on a mountainside in an unexplored part of the moon—and realizes that Someone Has Been There Already.

In "The Sentinel," Clarke appeals to us on two levels, one straightforward, the other transcendental. On the straightforward level, SF readers who have an appetite for space stuff enjoy the description of everyday life on the moon. The narrator is part of an expedition exploring the Mare Crisium:

> As I stood by the frying-pan, waiting, like any terrestrial housewife, for the sausages to brown, I let my gaze wander idly over the mountain wall which covered the whole of the southern horizon, marching out of sight to the east and west below the curve of the Moon. They seemed only a mile or two from the tractor, but I knew that the nearest was twenty miles away. On the Moon, of course, there is no loss of detail with distance—none of that almost imperceptible haziness which softens and sometimes transfigures all far-off things on Earth.

The simple wonder of looking out of the window and seeing the mountains of the Moon in all their splendor is pleasurable and satisfying, giving the quality of Clarke's descriptive prose (he writes with real affection) and given that such description is relevant to an effectively plotted story. But in the end of the story, Clarke opens out with a transcendent sweep into something far more exciting than moon scenery; he suggests that the pyramid is a device for sending signals, planted in the knowledge that humanity would discover it if and when they evolved and matured enough to travel into space. And that humanity will try to take it apart to see how it works and in doing so, destroy it—so the pyramid will stop sending out signals. Which will itself be the signal to the older race that it is time to come see what's happening on Earth.

The story ends with the narrator looking up at the sky: "I do not think we will have to wait for long." Science at its boldest is not mere rationality but the means to step into the larger Unknown. Clarke uses this awareness to write stories that send cosmic chills down our spines.

This is the kind of idea for which science fiction is famous, plots that can be summarized and still transmit the essential chill—what a fantastic idea—big, wonderful, mind-stretching.

These are ideas from the wellsprings of science and technology made flesh and hooked into the rest of existence to give them thematic reverberations. This is what science fiction does. And the ideas intersect with the real, mundane world through whatever thematic material the writer can provide to sound great bells.

3 | Worshiping at the Church of Wonder

The question of science fiction and religion has been raised frequently since the 1950s. Before that there was no question, since it had been settled in the late nineteenth century that science and religion were unalterably opposed. And the writers of science fiction, beginning at the time of H. G. Wells, had not dealt with the subject except, infrequently, to portray religious characters as "the opposition." A whole body of clichés (e.g., the repressive religious dictatorship, antiscientific and antihumanistic, found in Heinlein's Future History series or in Fritz Leiber's *Gather, Darkness*) dominated American SF for decades. The other side of the coin, the idea of a new "scientific religion," occurs in the field infrequently, in fringe-area works such as M. P. Shiel's *The Last Miracle* and L. Ron Hubbard's controversial Dianetics (a discipline now known as Scientology). Certainly the works of David Lindsay (especially *A Voyage to Arcturus*) and later C. S. Lewis are intimately involved with religious questions, but these are generally isolated examples far from the main body and traditions of popular science fiction prior to the mid-1950s.

However, in the place of religion per se there was a tradition of wonder and transcendence at the very heart of the SF field from Wells, Olaf Stapledon, Blish, and Clarke to E. E. Smith, John W. Campbell, Robert A. Heinlein, Ray Bradbury, A. E. Van Vogt, and Isaac Asimov. One might even say that to the members of the SF field, there was and is an anagogical level present in SF literature.

I am not going to pursue those particular works of SF that deal with theology and dispute, though many of them are among the generally acknowledged masterpieces of SF, from Clarke's "The Star" and Blish's *A Case of Conscience* through Walter M. Miller's *A Canticle for Leibowitz* to the later works of Philip K. Dick. These are often discussed in courses on SF and religion for the purpose of illuminating religion, not SF. I propose to use religion to discuss SF, as an approach to what readers get from it and how.

A SENSE of wonder, awe at the vastness of space and time, is at the root of the excitement of science fiction. Any child who has looked up at the stars at night and thought about how far away they are, how there is no end or outer edge to this place, this universe—any child who has felt the thrill of fear and excitement at such thoughts stands a very good chance of becoming a science fiction reader.

To say that science fiction is in essence a religious literature is an overstatement, but one that contains truth. SF is a uniquely modern incarnation of an ancient tradition: the tale of wonder. Tales of miracles, tales of great powers and consequences beyond the experience of people in your neighborhood, tales of the gods who inhabit other worlds and sometimes descend to visit ours, tales of humans traveling to the abode of the gods, tales of the uncanny: all exist now as science fiction.

Science fiction's appeal lies in its combination of the rational, the believable, with the miraculous. It is an appeal to the sense of wonder.

Science fiction has about it an extraliterary quality. Most SF stories that lack literary distinction—all the average and below average tales that comprise the bulk of the field—can be summarized as well as or better than they read in full text. What is attractive to the sense of wonder may be evinced in a single paragraph or outline, just as the power and wonder of an ancient Greek myth is communicated in summary form. Certainly an excellent SF story, just like an excellent literary version of one of the Greek myths, has powerful and complex virtues not available in summary. But the wonder is not necessarily lost or absent in a not-very-literate popular telling. The crude level of style and the pulp storytelling conventions did not prevent the earliest Gernsbackian SF from filling its audience with wonder.

Wonder stories of science and technology go back at least to the late eighteenth century and progress in various forms through Sebastien Mercier and Voltaire, Mary Wollstonecraft Shelley and Poe (and a very large number of others in France, Germany, England, and America) to Verne and Wells.

Jules Verne was the first writer to make his name almost entirely from the production of this kind of story. For a hundred years, readers of Verne have thrilled to the wonder of a voyage to the moon in a capsule shot from a huge cannon; of a journey through the caverns underneath an extinct volcano into the depths of the Earth; of a trip undersea, filled with adventures, in an enormous submarine. These stories have sunk their hooks deep into the consciousness of a large number of readers, some of whom became SF writers in later decades. Verne's influence on SF cannot be overstated; he was the first to produce a whole body of work about the wonders of science.

H. G. Wells began writing while Verne was still active, and produced his last major SF work, *Things to Come,* ten years after Hugo Gernsback founded *Amazing Stories.* The power of Wells's early novels, *The Time Machine, The War of the Worlds, The First Man in the Moon,* and *The Island of Dr. Moreau,* and of his many short stories, makes him the crucial writer linking Verne and modern SF. He was a writer with literary virtues lacking in Verne, but his other talents pale in the light of his ability to envision things and ideas that excite wonder: the time machine itself, and the beauties and terrors of the future; a war on Earth with invading intelligent beings from another planet; a visit to an alien civilization on the moon; the creation of beast-men; the incursion into our daily lives of astronomical events ("The Star" and *In the Year of the Comet*). His later extrapolative novels, such as *When the Sleeper Wakes, A Modern Utopia* and *The War in the Air,* provided fodder for the minds of Gernsback and his first generation of readers and writers (in fact, generations raised on Verne and Wells were the core of Gernsback's audience), as well as a technique for creating future worlds that has dominated the SF field since his day.

But Gernsback was an inventor, obsessed with technology, and it was Verne and the followers of Verne, in the dime novels and boys' books such as the Tom Swift series with their wonderful machines, who initially influenced the new field and astounded and delighted the audience. The early issues of *Amazing Stories*, with their blazing, glowing covers of strange worlds and creatures and of cataclysmic events, delivered the technological miracles of the future. It was not until the mid-1930s that the Wellsian influence began to dominate the field.

Meanwhile, there were two authors, rarely discussed today, whose work dominated the SF field and who contributed romance and adventure mixed with color and strangeness: Edgar Rice Burroughs and E. E. Smith, Ph.D.

Burroughs was one of the world's most popular adventure writers from 1914 onward, and the major portion of his work aside from the Tarzan books was one variety of SF or another: his Martian adventures and his Pellucidar books, *Carson of Venus* and the world "at the Earth's core." Although most of his work appeared in the adventure pulps such as *Argosy* and *Blue Book*, Gernsback did get *Master Minds of Mars* for *Amazing Annual*.

"Doc" Smith, batter chemist for a doughnut manufacturer, who had written a romance of space travel in 1919 but never sold it, found a market for *The Skylark of Space* in *Amazing Stories*, and for the first time catapulted humanity in spaceships beyond the solar system out into the galaxy and beyond, there to meet strange races both good and evil. Smith widened the possibilities of SF and remained the most popular author in the field right until the advent of Heinlein, Asimov, Van Vogt, and the rest in John W. Campbell's *Astounding.* Campbell's own writing career began as author of rousing interstellar adventures in emulation of Smith—and his name was so identified with those adventures that when he began in the mid 1930s to write intense, atmospheric Wellsian SF, he used the pseudonym Don A. Stuart.

Neither Burroughs nor Smith had any literary pretensions. They were popular writers of pulp adventure, knew it, and gloried in it. Burroughs's SF had a wider audience because all his works were immediately put into hardcover, but within the burgeoning field Smith was the greatest. And for one reason only: His stories struck the sense of wonder like lightning. His huge, galactic, cosmic adventures were electrifyingly new. After reading Smith, you could look up at the night sky as never before, and be filled with a whole new range of awesome potentialities.

The writer of science fiction could expand his consciousness into new ranges of possibilities, obtain totally new perspectives, see new visions. And the readers, the first generation of omnivores, became chronic omnivores—after all, it was then possible to read literally all SF published and catch up on the classics of Verne and Wells and still have time left for other reading. For the first time ever, after the existence of *Amazing Stories,* you could identify yourself to others as a fan of that particular kind of literature, correspond with others of like mind, and proselytize.

Young men such as Jack Williamson and Ed Hamilton got published in *Amazing Stories* and founded careers with the intention of writing this new kind of fiction. Most of their stories were rough or crude or cliché-ridden, or all that and more; but they had the addiction and knew what the readers wanted—action, excitement, cosmic ideas. And they knew that the action and excitement, although necessary, were not the real point. The crux of every story had to be the aspect that sparked the sense of wonder. That was what differentiated the "scientifiction" readership from all other pulp adventure readers.

All the works of Smith and all of Burroughs's SF are still in print in paperback and are reissued regularly with new packages—probably the best evidence of their enduring popularity and of the success with which they still inspire wonder, regardless of archaic clichés, outdated science, and just plain bad writing.

To this day some of the best SF is not terribly well written. A sensitive reader of fiction must put aside literary fashion and prejudices against "bad writing," even with some of the classics of science fiction, if he hopes to understand what attracts so many seemingly intelligent people. Of course even today a majority of the readers of SF have no literary sophistication or are style deaf or both; but this has helped the field immeasurably during its formative decades, when it served raw unprepared wonder in unassimilated lumps, when no one ever let the writing get in the way of the cosmic and awesome ideas.

There is a substantial amount of fine writing that is also good SF now. Even though a whole lot of people in the field would rather not admit any longer that wonder is still the crucial element of success in SF, it is and will remain so as long as the field survives. After all, very few of the SF adventure novels of the Thirties and Forties are out of print in paperback in the 1980s—at least not for long. Wonder endures.

Obviously SF does not have a corner on wonder—certain works of fantasy and supernatural horror have a similar ability to arouse fear, delight, and awe (and, as we noted earlier, those works tend to be written by writers who also write SF). Much more rarely, one finds modern or contemporary fiction that evokes mystery and wonder. Such works have not been common since the 1920s outside the borders of fantasy and science fiction except in children's literature—here fantasy abounds but is not constrained into conventional limitations of any sort, from Oz and Winnie the Pooh and Lang's fairy books through Saint-Exupéry and Thurber and many others to the present. Luckily for the SF field, the children raised on this literature are ripe for the wonders of SF, a repository of potential omnivores and chronics.

Science fiction has claimed the domains of time (especially the distant future) and space, the infinite possibilities out there, just at the moment when the last locations of awe and mystery have disappeared from our planet—terra incognita, distant islands, forbidden Tibet, the mysterious East. And recently the possibility of alternate universes, including an infinity of possible pasts and presents, is being claimed by SF. Except for the imaginary past of classical or other, such as Arthurian, mythology, science fiction has most of the territory. SF ranges free through the infinite spaces and times, finding and focusing on the nodes that inspire wonder—catastrophes, big events, the supernal beauties of cosmic vistas, endless opportunities for new and strange experiences that astound and illuminate. This is the point Campbell was addressing when he asserted that all the rest of literature is just a special case of SF, while SF is broader and freer than any other writing. The territory is huge.

The readers want it huge too, and want it always expanding. In the 1920s, they clamored for more Doc Smith, and *Amazing* convinced him to write a sequel to his original novel. *Skylark Three* was filled with "a stupendous panorama of alien life-forms, mile-long spaceships travelling faster than light, devastating ray-weapons, and frightful battles in the void ending in inevitable triumphs for the visiting Earthmen" (Gillings, *The Best of E. E. "Doc" Smith,* London: Weidenfeld & Nicholson, 1975, p. 11). Then in 1931, after Gernsback had left *Amazing Stories* to found *Science Wonder Stories* and *Air Wonder Stories,* Smith came up with another story, *Spacehounds of IPC,* which confined his heroes of the Inter-Planetary Corporation to the solar system. This, he insisted, was true scientific fiction, not pseudoscience, and he planned to make it the first of a series— but it wasn't what his fans wanted: "We want Smith to write stories of scope and range. We want more Skylarks!" was the cry. And *Amazing*'s eighty-year-old editor, Dr. T. O'Conor Sloane, who still had seven years to go before he retired, pointed a lean finger out towards the Milky Way" (*The Best of E. E. Smith,* p. 11).

But as H. G. Wells maintained in his famous introduction to his collected early novels, where everything is possible, nothing is particularly interesting or wonderful. So the challenge to the wondermakers who have written SF has been to set limits acceptable to their audiences and, presumably, based on knowledge of science, then to push on to the very edges of those limits (or, carefully and with respect, to break them) to create wonder.

It is entirely the task of the writer to limit the work, since such enormous freedom is granted by the audience.

So there has always existed from the time of Smith a dynamic and fruitful tension between writer and audience in science fiction, between the author's need to control the matter of science fiction and the audience's insatiable desire for more marvels. And in the end the audience has always triumphed. It is an audience thoroughly experienced in the work of the field, knowledgeable, jaded even, which has pressed the authors of science fiction continually for newer, bigger, better tales of wonder, more fantastic worlds and astounding stories—more excess, more often than not.

It is not surprising, then, that from the 1920s onward, science fiction writers have eagerly incorporated other related subgenres such as utopias and dystopias, stories of lost races, mythologies, marvelous voyages, and indeed all of literary fantasy. And it cannot be surprising that such an acquisitive agglomeration should resist definition, since each successful story contributes to a redefinition of the field's boundaries. Given the mandates of the loyal, vocal core audience, with its traditions of immediate feedback to the writers, the pressure to be creative is always on a writer of science fiction.

And to turn the coin over, the pressure is always on the author to repeat past triumphs. The lesser talents have solved this problem by hacking out variations on the creative successes of their earlier work or the SF stories of others—but the audience has usually been able to spot the difference between creative emulation (which they like and support) and cliché repetition. They will support an entire career that is devoted to wringing every last drop of essential wonder from an original idea complex (Doc Smith wrote only two substantial series of novels over his five decades in the field) but will withdraw support and approval from any writer, no matter how talented his execution, who fails them by turning attention away from the marvelous. They are particularly resistant to and suspicious of stylistic sophistication or experimentation unless it is clearly in support of some wondrous effect. They are the children of H. G. Wells, not Henry James.

To the uninitiated observer, one of the most difficult perceptions to grasp is that the SF audience is just as important as the writers and the written work to an understanding of science fiction. Why is the fiction often so badly written but seemingly praised and honored by its devotees? Because the execution is secondary to the wonder aroused by it. Why are science fiction writers, a noticeably bright and creative lot, so paranoiac about the lack of serious attention paid their works outside SF? Because they know that only the very best of them can satisfy the demands of their audience and also pull off the trick of writing according to present literary fashion (which is of course irrelevant to their supporting audience).

Science fiction is as much a phenomenon as it is a body of written work; outsiders are in the position of the blind men in the fable of the blind men and the elephant: They tend to arrive at generalizations based on parts, not the whole. But the evidence is all there, in the books and magazines, the fanzines, histories, social events, reference books. The science fiction field worships wonder.

A pointed example of the modern wonder-story is Larry Niven's 1972 Hugo award-winning "Inconstant Moon." The evening I first read the story in 1971, I thought, This story is going to win the Hugo! Even if history had proved that wrong, what I knew in a moment was that "Inconstant Moon" would delight chronic readers of SF.

This is "Inconstant Moon": A lover stands on a balcony looking up at the moon as lovers do. The moon grows brighter and brighter as he watches, and his present joy turns to awe and fear as he reasons it out, for now it casts a glow as bright as full daylight and he knows that a transcendent catastrophe is occurring, the sun increasing its brightness many times over, and that humanity may have only hours to live. As the world turns toward dawn, the man and his girlfriend spend their brief hours in a night of frantic romance as tension mounts—until, with dawn approaching, the moon fades back to normal. A solar flare, not a nova! Our lovers will have a fighting chance to survive, though the daylight side of the Earth must surely have been destroyed. They begin to plan for the future.

The nightmare vision of that uncanny moon is as powerful an image as was ever projected by a work of science fiction. You must know something of high school astronomy to get the idea immediately, but any chronic or omnivore of science fiction is so charged by that image that he may reimagine it at will without rereading the entire story and still get the thrill of wonder.

This is a crucial point in our discussion of what SF is all about. You must understand that a constant desire for arousal, for that electric input that charges the "wonder sense," is what really hooks people on science fiction and makes omnivores into chronics. The science fiction person would rather read a story that alerts and strokes this sense than anything else. Anything. He would rather read (or reread, after a time) "Inconstant Moon" than any work of fiction, no matter how perceptive and carefully written, polished and artful, that does not arouse wonder.

Chronics are patient and determined. They spend years reading SF regularly and frequently, supporting specialized magazines and large publishing programs, seeking and constantly finding stories that ignite wonder.

It looks strange to an outsider, but perhaps you should think of it this way: A chronic reading science fiction is more like one of the faithful attending a church service than an experienced critic responding to a work of art. The act of reading SF continually provides access to wonder, just as the church service provides access to worship.

But an outsider doesn't gain access easily. Walk into the temple of a religion other than yours and feel discomfort and, perhaps, disorientation. Or, better, consider the situation of a child in the cathedral of her parents' faith—she must spend years of training in the symbology of the religion before she has access to the awe and wonder of it. Until then it is just a big, fancy room with strange decorations.

Beyond the actual is the realm of wonder and the mysterious. Who would deny the existence of mysteries, or their power over human life and civilization? Young people search for mystery to inform and validate their lives; older people venerate the mysteries they have confronted, shape their lives around the attempt to penetrate the mysteries they perceived or stumbled upon in their youth. Mysteries stimulate the heart, the will, and the imagination toward something beyond day-to-day survival.

For many young people today, science fiction stories in all their variety take the place of religious texts from times gone by, stimulating their readers to take interest in and hunger for something larger than mundane life, for a life lit by the glow of wonder. And it is not uncommon for a young omnivore to become derailed from science fiction by precisely the arousal of wonder. Joanna Russ relates that one of her students explained how reading Arthur C. Clarke's *Childhood's End* had awakened her religious feelings and led her to join the Catholic church (this caused by an SF novel about humanity evolving into an ultimate being of pure group mind). Enough people who are influential in religious education have perceived dimly enough this connection between SF and religion to create a fair number of courses around the U.S. in SF and religion. Most of them, however, make the elementary mistake of teaching only SF works that are *about* religion, thereby directing the students' attention away from whatever point there might be.

One story to have received such treatment is Arthur C. Clarke's 1953 classic, "The Nine Billion Names of God." Toward the end of this short piece of brilliant plotting, two rational computer engineers aboard a plane leaving a lamasery high in the Himalayas have discussed the quaint but threatening attempts of a religious sect in the East that hired them to use a computer to help fulfill God's purpose for mankind—to list all the possible names of God and thereby find the real name, after which the world will end (as a prelude to something bigger). They are on their way home as the contract is completed by the computer below. One engineer, George, remarks that the computer run must be ending about now just as Chuck notices that outside ("without any fuss") the stars in the sky are beginning to go out!

Of course, science fiction can be used for purposes other than its own, and often is, by everyone from futurologists and sociologists to physicists. (At a recent academic conference, the annual Modern Language Association meeting, a couple of physicists spoke on using SF to teach physics—Hugo Gernsback would have been delighted.) But to teach such an SF story as

"The Nine Billion Names of God" as anything other than a story about the sense of wonder is narrow and, we suspect, just the kind of reduction of literature to "teachability" that discourages students from reading on their own for whatever range of pleasure literature offers. To use science fiction is, most often, to abuse it. So it is a common complaint of SF chronics and omnivores, which we will discuss in a later chapter, that science fiction courses are a danger to the field, at best irrelevant, at worst pernicious and perverse.

Science fiction stories are performances, just like the Christian mystery plays of the Middle Ages. In the mystery plays, full of miracles and wondrous paradoxes (he was dead and yet he lives, a virgin has borne a child), the audience experienced in vivid and dramatic reenactment the wonders of their faith, and their religious feelings were aroused and celebrated. The original location of the plays, the ministerium (church), from which they took their name, changed over the course of time to the streets and the word "mystery" came to signify the wonders and miracles presented. So "science fiction" has come to signify, for the field, stories that arouse "sense of wonder." A science fiction story clothes and enacts in narrative a wonder.

A useful example of the consciousness through which a science fiction writer creates an embodiment of wonder is the story (and the circumstances by which the story came to be) "Nightfall," by Isaac Asimov. It is often pointed to as perhaps the greatest of the classic SF stories of Campbell's "golden age." When the Science Fiction Writers of America voted in 1965 to establish the contents of the definitive science fiction anthology to that date, "Nightfall" received the most votes of all for inclusion in *The Science Fiction Hall of Fame*:

On a distant planet orbiting a complex system of six multiple suns, so that total darkness occurs anywhere on the planet only every two thousand and forty-nine years, astronomers predict that such a darkness can and will happen, only to be ridiculed by their two-thousand-year-old society. A certain nut cult has a tradition that civilization is cyclic and ends in darkness every 2,050 years—no one else takes the astronomers' prediction seriously: No living human is psychologically capable of withstanding real darkness. And then, as night begins to fall, the entire race, which never had the need to invent artificial light, goes mad from fear and begins to light great fires, burning down their civilization in order to escape the dark. With nightfall, the race is reduced to madness and barbarism, doomed by its own psychology.

In *The Early Asimov* (New York: Doubleday, 1972, p. 319) Isaac Asimov recalls entering John W. Campbell's office with a story idea that was instantly rejected because Campbell had just come across a quotation from Ralph Waldo Emerson: "If the stars should appear one night in a thousand years, how would men believe, and adore, and preserve for many generations the remembrance of the city of God!"

> Campbell asked me what I thought would happen if the stars would appear at only very long intervals. I had nothing intelligent to suggest.
>
> "I think men would go mad," he said thoughtfully.
>
> We talked about that notion for quite a while, and I went home to write a story on the subject, one that Campbell and I decided from the start was to be called "Nightfall."

To say that the situation outlined is a uniquely successful example of editor and author arriving at a commercial idea and that the professional environment of the science fiction writer and editor has always encouraged such interactions (remember Sloan and Doc Smith) does not penetrate beyond the surface of this example. The unspoken and a priori agreement between Asimov and Campbell was that they were engaged in a continuing enterprise with rather specific goals: to search out peculiarly science fictional story ideas, ideas that, when cast in story form, would not merely be clever and effective but would also satisfy the desire for arousal of a sense of wonder through the impact of their range and scope. They knew that what they were doing was serious and important.

Am I kidding? Serious and important? You bet! John W. Campbell was one of the most successful and innovative practicing science fiction writers when he agreed by contract with the publisher of *Astounding* never to publish any fiction during his editorship. Rather than work to support himself elsewhere while he wrote, he chose to edit because he had a powerful and

serious vision of the greater potentialities of science fiction—
and he used his editorship to create this greater flowering. He
committed the rest of his life to the task. And Isaac Asimov,
from his early teens an avid reader of science fiction and
member of the famous Futurians (the New York City SF fan
club that included Fred Pohl, Donald Wollheim, Cyril Kornbluth, and later James Blish, Damon Knight, and Judith Merril—read the fascinating, gossipy history of the group, *The
Futurians,* by Damon Knight), was a young man whose whole
personality had been formed by his association with science
fiction. They certainly were not in it for the money. They were
part of the elect.

This feeling of importance and seriousness is expressed over
and over: "The humble truth is that science fiction is only for
the small number of people who like to think and who regard
the universe with awe, which is a blend of love and fear. 'The
public' does neither; it wants to be spoon-fed by its magazines
and movies, and it regards the universe with horror, which is a
blend of fear and hate" (Knight, *In Search of Wonder,* rev. and
enl. ed., Chicago: Advent, 1967; pp. 277–78). The demands that
science fiction makes on the chronic and omnivore—of reading,
with unflagging enthusiasm, through the bad stuff to find the
good stuff, always open and responding though often dissatis-
fied; of loyalty and faith—are worth it because the quest is
important. Loyal and faithful reading is the act of worship.

I have spoken earlier about big ideas and the importance of
scale in science fiction, of great distances and spans of time,
huge objects and vast importances ("Only one man in all the
universe could combat the menace . . ."). It is the intention of
science fiction to heighten and intensify, to highlight and cast
in relief whatever matter the individual story chooses. Science
fiction is by nature symbolic at the same moment that it is
logical and rational. The impact of "Nightfall" or "Inconstant
Moon," so logically and carefully grounded, is beyond the
rational and in the realm of awe.

Let us examine Arthur C. Clarke's well-known dictum on the
importance of point of view: He states that a technology that is
sufficiently advanced beyond our present state of knowledge
would be indistinguishable from magic, just as lighting a match

would be considered an act of magic if it were witnessed by a human from a primitive culture. The science fiction reader asks of a story that it reveal an act of such magic and, according to the field's conventions, explain the magic, usually as technology. What makes the story SF is not the magic but the explanation that suggests that the magic is actually possible. We are given an explanation that does not destroy the magic ("it was only a dream") but rather promises the possibility of that particular magic, perhaps far away in space, or in the future.

Science fiction promises wonder outside the confines and limitations of the story. The wonder we perceive in the story could be real in a faraway place, or might be real someday. Science fiction delivers us from the written page into a universe of wonder infinitely renewed. It is the transcendence of the written page that is at the core of the appeal of science fiction. Science fiction makes *us* transcendent. That is why we keep returning to the analogy of science fiction and religion, to the extraliterary appeal.

C. S. Lewis, in his *An Experiment in Criticism* (England: Cambridge University Press, 1961), develops an unusual and relevant argument: In an attempt to combat the narrowing elitism and swings of fashion with which criticism has beset literature and the readers in modern times, he characterizes the "unliterary" reader of fiction as attracted to fiction in three ways: by excitement—imminent dangers and hair-breadth escapes, the continual winding up and relaxing of (vicarious) anxiety; by arousing curiosity, prolonging, exasperating, and finally satisfying it ("Hence the popularity of stories with a mystery in them. This pleasure is universal and needs no explanation. It makes a great part of the philosopher's, the scientist's, or the scholar's happiness. Also of the gossip's."); and by success stories ("They like stories which enable them—vicariously, through the characters—to participate in pleasure or happiness," p. 37).

But we should not make the facile connection between science fiction and what Lewis refers to as "bad books" (the opposite of "good books"). Lewis maintains that a good book is one that may be read by a good reader—a provocative assertion, to which Lewis devotes the support of his impressive learning and talents.

Science fiction is for the most part read by readers who, *when they are reading anything other than science fiction,* fall quite comfortably into Lewis's character of the unliterary reader. When an omnivore or chronic reads a science fiction story, however, the case is different, as different as, say, the response of an American baseball fan to a World Series game as opposed to his reaction to a test match in cricket. Or if you consider that analogy too extreme, then consider the disparity between the response of a sophisticated reader of fiction to a short story versus a work of contemporary poetry (which is read, sadly, by few who are not poets). All too many readers of fiction find it unruly nonsense, impenetrable. I maintain that a science fiction person reading a science fiction story interacts with that story in a rich and complex way, purposeful and meaningful.

Lewis goes on to devote an entire chapter ("On Myth") to the kind of story with which contemporary criticism is poorly equipped to deal. The myth (Lewis is using the word "myth" in a generalized sense from its root meaning in Greek: story) has six salient features:

1. It is extraliterary in the sense that a bare outline or summary communicates a powerful impression to any person of sensibility. Lewis demonstrates that this is not true of good literary works, using examples from *The Odyssey* to *Middlemarch.*
2. The pleasure of myth depends hardly at all on the usual narrative attractions of suspense or surprise. It is a permanent object of contemplation, more like a thing than a narration.
3. Human sympathy is at a minimum. We do not project ourselves strongly into the inner life of the characters. "We feel indeed that the pattern of their movements has a profound relevance to our own life, but we do not imaginatively transport ourselves into theirs." (This is true of some great science fiction but not by any means all—some SF does have the literary virtues of characterization, e.g., the novels of Philip K. Dick).

4. These stories are always fantastic. They deal with impossibles and preternaturals.

5. The experience may be sad or joyful but it is always serious ("grave").

6. The experience is not only serious but awe-inspiring. "We feel it to be numinous. It is as if something of great moment had been communicated to us."

Thus Lewis establishes a framework of considerable import for the consideration of science fiction.

Following this, Lewis discusses the difference between the unliterary reader and the extraliterary reader, which points directly to our characterization of the SF reader (p. 46):

> The man who first learns what is to him a great myth through a verbal account which is baldly or vulgarly or cacophonously written, discounts and ignores the bad writing and attends solely to the myth. He hardly minds about the writing. He is glad to have the myth on any terms. But this would seem to be almost exactly the same behavior which . . . I attributed to the unliterary. In both there is the same minimum attention to the words and the same concentration on the Event (what happens). Yet if we equated the lover of myth with the mass of the unliterary we should be deeply mistaken.

Of course it may be that the words that tell the story are in themselves a fine work of literary art. When this happens, the SF field rejoices in the attention paid by outsiders to that work and is dismayed that those same outsiders cannot appreciate the appeal and virtues of the rest of science fiction merely because it is not quite so well written. The extraliterary pleasure is the real and true value of all the works to the initiated.

Since the 1930s, writing about SF by insiders has been filled with assertions that the essence of science fiction is "wonder," but not one of these discussions has made itself intelligible to nonreaders of science fiction. Indeed, a majority of the books and essays on science fiction have been so myopic that they have been ridiculed within large portions of SF itself. I have experienced decades of discussion with people exposed to science fiction only through media sci-fi whose perception of science fiction was incoherent but favorable—they like to be massaged by SF. And I have experienced of course more and necessarily shorter conversations with people who know nothing about SF *and* know they wouldn't like it. My inevitable conclusion has been that there are so many barriers set up in contemporary society to keep individuals away from the experience of aroused wonder that the messianic impulse of so many SF chronics and omnivores is doomed with adults generally.

I am attempting here a sufficient distance from science fiction in order to combine and resolve images of the field, examining both the preconceptions of insiders and outsiders for the illumination of both. There is perhaps more nonsense spoken about science fiction than any other variety of narrative. The sheer amount of noise generated by and about SF over the years should have signaled perceptive outsiders that here is something that ought to be examined and understood. That you are reading this sentence indicates an awareness that civilization in the 1980s has somehow been influenced by science fiction. Perhaps even that your own circumstances or personality as a child have been so influenced—can you remember what the effect of science fiction was on you?

Science fiction can and does create transformations into the mythic for our culture. Every chronic reader of SF knows this, just as he knows certain things about the shape of our future and about the attractions of SF that no one ever seems to have been able to communicate to outsiders.

And so, in a sense, the chronics have built walls around themselves, invented the whole paraphernalia of SF fandom to protect their access to these myths, these wonder stories, and to keep outsiders from positions of power in the SF community— this includes critics, publishers, all those who would abuse SF by using it as some sort of device, or who would somehow obscure or compromise the essential core of wonder. Paranoia and idealism have always been among the most salient characteristics of the science fiction community.

The congregation, Damon Knight's "small number of people" (with its distant echoes of the Miltonic "fit audience, though few"), still worships at the church of wonder—but you can't come in unless you join.

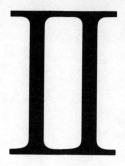

II | EXPLORING THE WORLDS OF SF

4 Running Away from the Real World

Perhaps the most common term used these days for what we seek in the popular arts is "escape," a word ordinarily implying condescension or contempt. Yet, though C. S. Lewis was once moved to observe that the only people to whom the word "escape" is a pejorative are jailers, it is hard to use it as an honorific.   —Leslie A. Fiedler, *What Was Literature?*

OKAY, you are now twelve years old and you have made a discovery that at least temporarily will change your life: You have found science fiction in written form. You have known SF from TV cartoons since you were two years old and could hardly say "Popeye" or "Bugs Bunny." You have seen it in comic books, played with SF toys, and watched monster movies—all the normal elements of kid culture. But now you have discovered something more intense and wonderful, the real SF. And it transports you out of the problem-filled, adult-controlled world of the kid into alternate universes.

Sure, reading is good for you and yes, you do learn something of science and logic, but this stuff is not popular science writing: This is fiction—this is escape! The excitement of escape is what creates SF omnivores. The world of SF is not just different, it is better than reality, and you want to escape to it as often as possible.

All of us have problems in the real world that we are incapable of solving. We perceive a disparity between how we would like things to be and how they are. At age twelve, most of our desires, the solutions to most of our problems, lie in the future when we will know more, understand more, be more in control of ourselves and our destiny. SF takes us to a multiplicity of futures. Vonnegut remarked, apropos of escape, that science fiction and pornography offer in common an escape from our real and unsolvable problems into an impossibly hospitable world.

The further discovery by some omnivores of an actual community of SF writers and readers that they can join may well represent utopia here and now. We have seen that the science fiction environment, at conventions and through amateur magazines, is hospitable to individuals with minor or major problems of social adjustment (something American culture in the latter half of the twentieth century allows too little room for in general now that the small town and local church environments have shrunk into comparative obscurity). The SF world awaits you if you choose.

So it is no wonder that one of the central appeals of science fiction is the myth of a better future, especially a future in which problems are solved or solvable through science and the application of logic, a future you can find yourself participating in through the story. This is a future in which you can be larger than life, a variety of superman or wonder woman—yes, it is wish-fulfillment, but it is better and more convincing than a magic kiss that turns you into a prince, froggie. It seems convincing for the duration because the question of how all these wishes might actually be fulfilled through science is addressed.

Over his decades of influence, John W. Campbell devoted much editorial verbiage to tying SF to problem-solving. "Convince me," he said to his writers, "that the problem you have posed in the story is solvable and that the manner of the solution is possible." By saying this, he was articulating and reinforcing one of the foundations of all SF: It has to be possible, so the reader's suspension of disbelief is not betrayed.

But let us not put too much weight on this aspect of the escape into SF, because in the omnivore stage, a person will read anything he can get his hands on, no matter how weak or strong the underpinnings. Every story is new, different, appealing because the offer is eternally renewed: Come to the future where things are exciting; you don't have to wait for it to come to you.

It is easier for a reader today than it used to be, too. Almost any older chronic reader of SF will tell you tales of the old days, when a twelve-year-old had to hide an SF book or magazine from parents, teachers, even friends, because it was universally known to be damaging trash only a small step above porn. Brain rot. You had to take it as your personal thing and have the courage to keep buying it and reading it (ah, secret thrill) and hiding it. Of such shared experiences are revolutionary cadres welded together. The early SF fan clubs seem to have felt this intense sense of shared escape. Now we are laid back.

Science fiction has been accused of being escapist literature. It sure is. Judith Merril and her cohort SF writers of the Fifties were creating seeds of change, using SF ideas to alter the present and create a more desirable future. One implication of that conscious effort is that the writers were unsatisfied with their present reality and actually planned an escape from it through their own creative efforts. The whole field, writers as well as fans, shared a need for change and a common bond through the awareness that SF really can affect the way things are and will be.

At least once in every decade, beginning with Hugo Gernsback in the 1920s, there has been a revolutionary impulse to create a better future through SF. The most recent cycle was the anti-New Wave/back-to-technological-optimism movement spearheaded by Lester del Rey in the 1970s, almost Gernsbackian in its thrust. This might seem more than a little absurd on the surface to an outsider involved in, say, social work or politics. But consider the influence of SF on a linguistic and conceptual level: The truly revolutionary act is writing it and reading it—especially reading it—through which our perception of reality is altered.

One reason it is so difficult for an outsider to communicate successfully with a person in the SF field is that SF insiders are living in a somewhat different reality, one that incorporates a spectrum of desirable (and undesirable) futures. Think of the old saw about university professors living in ivory towers isolated from the realities of daily life—well, SF people have escaped certain conceptual limitations that most outsiders suffer like horse-blinders, preventing them from seeing what is not smack in front of them. By means of SF reading, chronics have isolated themselves in a world of ideas, have built towers that afford them vistas beyond the mundane. They have little leverage in the great world of politics and commerce, but they can see for miles in many directions.

A twelve-year-old who has escaped the gym classes of daily life for exciting visions of the future has not lost anything in terms of potential adjustment to the real world. She may be an omnivore for several years and then venture fully into the outside world, pimples gone and breasts grown. But SF will ever after be accessible to her, and the vistas of the future she has seen remain, even if half forgotten. Escape is open to her. More than likely she can see further into the future than her parents and friends, and her behavior will be different because of it.

In a way, the dream of science fiction is to control reality by creating it. If you don't like the way things are, read a story about a world in which things are different. Be in that world. A long-term chronic, separated in some way from mundane life to begin with, does lose touch with many of the elements of daily life in the present, much like an absentminded professor—he is distracted by the future.

William Tenn, a leading SF humorist, stylist, and crazy idea-man, wrote an important essay on the art of science fiction as a preface to his first book, *Of All Possible Worlds* (Ballantine Books, 1955), in the course of which he attacked the frequent charge that SF is "escape literature." Tenn's argument is that all fiction is entertainment and that the purpose of entertainment is to draw the audience into a world other than the reality of the moment. Therefore all literature is escape, and the charge that escape is somehow pernicious is "a jealous argument of very ancient lineage indeed," used by "entrenched intellectual privilege" against popular literature from the time of Elizabethan drama to the present. And we might note that this argument has been used successfully in modern times to nearly eradicate adult fantasy from serious attention until very recently.

What has all this to do with *Star Wars, Star Trek, The Creature from the Black Lagoon, Buck Rogers,* pulp magazines, and John Carter of Mars? Tenn would say that escape entertainment can aspire to and become art. Okay, but there's nothing intrinsically wrong with plain old escape entertainment that doesn't aspire to art—much of written SF and all of media sci-fi. The science fiction audience wants escape—for good and sufficient reasons, as we have seen. If the escape mechanism happens to aspire to and in fact be literary art, all well and good; but we have investigated that already and know it is more or less irrelevant (remember Van Vogt, Doc Smith and the rest). It is outsiders who pretty much invariably and rigidly impose their standards and fashions on SF and find it wanting, much to the chagrin of writers such as Tenn.

For all that our center of focus has been the written SF of the last five decades, its nature and its appeal, we must spend a bit more time now on the other conduits through which SF ideas penetrate popular consciousness. Films, comics, toys, games, and pictorial art all contribute to the transmission and spread of SF in our culture. The purpose of all of these media forms is escape, entertainment, but this does not necessarily deprive them of power and influence. We have mentioned the creation of SF myths and referred to *Superman,* the *Star Trek* television series, and the proliferation of sci-fi movies in the 1950s. It would seem impossible for any adult in our culture to have escaped getting a visual impression of what SF "looks like" given the proliferation of the garish covers of magazines or paperbacks displayed everywhere in the nation for decades now. And what it looks like is romance, technology, fantasy. So this is what we get from the media—the package is the message.

No logic—logic's what you get in written form only. There are well-known stories in the lore of the SF field about film directors cutting out all the explanations and logic in favor of pacing and emotional impact of images. About the best thing an SF chronic has to say concerning sci-fi films and TV shows is that the best of them (some episodes of *Star Trek, The Invasion of the Body Snatchers, 2001*) at least allow you to imagine a reasonable SF explanation between the scenes without introducing illogical howlers.

The case of *Destination Moon* discussed earlier proved to the media that accuracy and trouble with detail is no more commercial than simply ignoring it all. The mass audience just doesn't care, as long as it is entertaining to them. But what has come through to mass audiences is a large variety of the crazy ideas of science fiction, making those ideas (spaceships, for instance) familiar. And the particular scientific and technological images of science fiction translated into visual forms have often proven striking and popular. Susan Sontag wrote an interesting essay on the monster films of the 1950s as "Cold War" myths. She pointed out the repetitive patterns in film after film, of a monster created or raised by the power of the atom that ultimately could be destroyed only by an atomic bomb or by "nature restoring the balance" (like the ending of H. G. Wells's *The War of the Worlds*).

That the moral or message of much sci-fi is diametrically opposed to that of written SF (reason, science, knowledge are worthwhile and effective in solving problems) does not at all relate to the general spread of images throughout our culture. These are now the images through which we confront reality, not escape from it. Whatever our philosophy or attitude, we now state our problems in terms of these images, so solutions must also come through them. We have escaped in the real world partly through media sci-fi into a new reality, the technology-filled world of the 1980s, and it is, of course, science fictional. Where do we escape to next?

Well, into the fiction again, into the far distance in time and space beyond the probability of the present catching up to the future. No matter where we are in reality, current science fiction is ranging beyond, by its very nature and the demands of the audience.

We have spoken of the distance between present reality and the world of an SF story, and of science fiction as a means of escape. But there is something paradoxical about this escape, for in a fair number of cases, distancing allows us to confront aspects of reality that we have no other means of approaching. Just as some sci-fi films embody a certain kind of contemporary truth (e.g., the "Cold War" myths), so SF can represent certain truths because *everyone knows* that what is said in SF is not true. This is one of the secrets of its attraction. The author of a science fiction story is free to tell the truth because everyone knows the story is not *real*. Thus in the era of Joe McCarthy, SF writers regularly portrayed and satirized the senator quite openly in SF stories, since the common knowledge that whatever they said couldn't be true protected them from political reprisals which were a clear and present threat to other writers.

If you start writing a factual article for *Newsweek* by saying, "Two out of every three people we see on the street are not real humans at all, but alien androids masquerading as people," you will be in trouble. You won't get past the first copy editor. You may not even get out of the building. If you begin a science fiction novel with the same words, however, you are on perfectly safe ground. Your novel will be published and quite a few of your readers will smile when they read your words *because they know them to be essentially true*. The chronics will be entertained by your ridiculously clear, daring statement of a commonly felt awareness.

In *Time Out of Joint* (1959), a novel by Philip K. Dick, Ragle Gumm in the middle of an ordinary day walks up to a hot dog stand when suddenly the place vanishes before his eyes, and all that's left where it used to be is a slip of paper with the words "hot dog stand" printed on it. At the end of the book, after a series of increasingly unnerving incidents like this one, and the development of quite a few subplots, we discover that our hero, Ragle, is not living in 1959 at all (as he had assumed) but in a construct of 1959 built for his benefit in 1995 as a means of overcoming his refusal to use his psychic powers against "the Enemy" in a war between Earth and its moon colony. While

Ragle thinks he is solving 1959 newspaper puzzles and winning prizes, he is actually predicting the landing sites of enemy missiles.

And any reader who has ever suspected that the world is an unreal construct built solely to deceive him has had a marvelous, hair-raising time learning that he's not really alone in his paranoia. The truths of science fiction are authentic somehow because they are built on outright lies. The authentic SF experience is a perception of truth, reality in an unreal environment. The immediate and clear presentation of the palpably untrue is a distancing device of great power and effectiveness. The radical distancing from quotidian reality frees the writer from many of the literary conventions through which reality is represented in mundane literature from Zane Grey to Saul Bellow. From this point of view, the science fictional world of the story is an unreal construct built to deceive the reader—and the reader eagerly penetrates the deceit to find the core of truth.

Now, the truths or kinds of truth the reader of SF finds in a story are not what she or he can find in other literature. Those conventions of representation used by writers from Grey to Bellow are finely tuned to illumine the daily details of human psychology and behavior under ordinary present or historical conditions (and indeed under many extraordinary conditions producing tension and abnormal behavior); the conventions aim at artful precision and verisimilitude. The SF writer may use some of these conventions but there is always a fundamental projection out of context—the world of the story is *not* real so that any word or words may have a new figurative or literal meaning in the new context. The last sentence of the Henry Kuttner story, "The Proud Robot," has a literal meaning impossible outside of SF: "Ten minutes later Gallagher was singing a duet with his can opener." Aside from the verbal delight, the pure play of words over the course of the story leading to the last line, the unusual and eccentric context (in this case the future world in which drunken Gallagher builds a narcissistic robot can opener) allows us to entertain possible modes of human behavior under circumstances which do not and have not ever applied in reality.

After all, the twelve-year-old omnivore of SF is put off by or bored with reality. He needs more than anything to put some distance between himself and the real world, which in many ways he is not equipped to handle. Aside from the social support of the SF field, he needs to experiment with experience, and written SF gives him worlds that he can play with. A twelve-year-old is not so much frightened of reality as bored by it—it is just there and he can't do anything about it. And one of the lessons of SF, as we have seen, is that you can manipulate reality, solve problems. There is hope in the future, as well as wonders and escape. The raw hope is enough for many early omnivores. In chronics, the escape into SF worlds often fosters an attitude we might call optimism tempered by irony, or hard-won optimism—no matter how bad the future is in story after story, at least it is there and, thank heavens, different from the present. Some few are even entertained by, in Brian W. Aldiss's phrase, "pure bracing gloom," which by contrast illuminates the virtues or acceptability of the everyday world.

You do not read SF to examine the nature of reality—that is just a by-the-way—you pick it up for escape and entertainment, and it draws you in and takes you away, there to perform strange and unnatural acts upon your mind. Science fiction has tremendous power over receptive minds and we have seen that our whole culture almost insures a certain amount of receptivity nowadays, in most kids.

In spite of this only a minority of twelve-year-olds read much SF, and until very recently (the last decade), mostly boys. After all, there is still that word "science" to discourage girls and there are still parents who insist that boys go outside and play, not read.

Of particular significance is the large increase of women readers of fantasy in the SF field in recent years. Unlike the chronics of older times, they will often happily admit to a casual dislike of anything with science in it and a strong bias in favor of any world, fantasy or futuristic, that represents strong and positive roles for women. Well and good, but general attitudes which involve fairly thorough rejection of the classics of the field are certainly going to produce and have already produced changes in SF. The new women writers of recent years have produced vigorous and innovative SF way out of proportion to their numbers.

It makes sense that most of the major new female SF writers of the 1970s—Suzy McKee Charnas, Vonda McIntyre, Elizabeth A. Lynn, Joan Vinge, Alice B. Sheldon, C. J. Cherryh, and many others—would have a desire to create new and different SF worlds; if not outright feminist futures, then certainly worlds in which women are highlighted and have serious and important new roles. Many women have turned to SF reading and writing because of the historic hospitality of the field toward change and innovation, and it is probably no overstatement to say that no woman in the SF field has remained unaffected by feminism in the 1970s.

Furthermore, the renewed passion of such diverse writers as Marion Zimmer Bradley, Joanna Russ, and Ursula K. Le Guin led them to create milestone works inspired by the burgeoning feminist consciousness of the 1970s. These three in particular, who had already made a significant impression on the field in the 1960s, came to real prominence in the 1970s and among them inspired much of the productive controversy of the decade.

The longings for future worlds of sexual equality and the sometimes violent rejection of the male-chauvinist present led to such works as Suzy McKee Charnas's *Motherlines* (1978); Joanna Russ's *The Female Man* (1975); Ursula K. Le Guin's *The Dispossessed* (1974) (her earlier *The Left Hand of Darkness* [1969] and Russ's *Picnic On Paradise* [1968] were the first important SF novels by women to reflect new attitudes toward sexual equality; Marion Zimmer Bradley's *The Heritage of Hastur* (1975); Alice B. Sheldon's (better known by her pseudonym, James Tiptree, Jr.) "The Women Men Don't See" (1976). Pamela Sargent's anthology, *Women of Wonder* (1975), proved so popular that it called forth two sequel volumes, making it the most popular SF reprint anthology of the decade. And these are only some of the high spots in a list that could be doubled or tripled in length. Male writers such as (in particular) John Varley and Samuel R. Delany also made significant contributions during the decade to the consideration of future sex roles.

It is worth noting that the most serious and fruitful intellectual inspiration and innovation in SF in recent years came from women and from the controversy surrounding the works of women writers. By the end of the 1970s, it was evident that women are the aliens in male-dominated human society, even in SF, and that the escape of women into SF worlds is of enormous personal and cultural significance for our immediate future.

It matters little that most of the women writing SF command popularity with only a minority of the total SF community. The source of the power of these new women writers in the SF field at present is that within their own core audience of (for the most part) adolescent and young women, they are transcendently heroic. Joanna Russ cannot appear in public at an SF convention without women coming up to her, a glaze of adulation in their eyes, to tell her how much she and her work mean to them, how it changed their lives—nor can Ursula K. Le Guin, nor Suzy McKee Charnas. These writers and their readers are the foremost current examples of science fiction as escape from an *intolerable* present day. They live in the SF world, correspond with one another, publish small-circulation magazines for each other discussing politics and life and the fiction of their courageous writers, who dare to envision and represent a world that is crucially different and better, a world they will make real.

There is also a strong, but harder to pinpoint, gay community within the SF field, both men and women, writers and readers, who are contributing to the free and innovative discussion of future sex roles. Again, the traditional openness of the field to personal freedom and the eccentricities of individuals has allowed the creation of futures with new and positive forms of human relations among people of varied sexual preferences. There are certain fanzines devoted in part to gay concerns, and the first full-scale bibliography on SF and gay themes, *Uranian Worlds* (Erik Garvin and Lyn Paleo, ed., Boston: G. K. Hall, 1983), is now available. SF is one of the first genres in which the cliché of the masculine hero versus the effeminate antagonist is no longer a requirement. Particularly significant contributions to the discussion of future sex roles began with Robert A. Heinlein's *Stranger in a Strange Land* (1961), no less than a full-scale satire on the sexual taboos of Western civilization, which became a bible of sexual freedom for the generation of the Sixties far outside the SF field. The works of Theodore Sturgeon, Philip Jose Farmer, Samuel R. Delany, Thomas M. Disch, Michael Moorcock, Joanna Russ, Marion Zimmer Bradley, and recently Elizabeth A. Lynn, among others, have carried on the theme of varieties of sexual activity in future worlds.

Perhaps the most complex and thorough presentation of varied sex roles in the SF of the 1970s occurs in Samuel R. Delany's *Dhalgren* (1975), one of the most popular SF books of the decade and perhaps the most controversial, since the world in the novel is not specifically juxtaposed to our present reality and contains events that are unexplained and surreal (Is it *really* SF?—the arguments rage on). Delany's novel is the most comprehensive sexual odyssey ever in the SF field and some of its power derives from the fact that the world of the book both is and is not present-day reality and that the sexual life of the characters is observed in clinical and objective graphic detail, cool and clear. For the SF field, *Dhalgren* is as revolutionary as Heinlein's novel—with the advent of Delany's masterpiece (the *New York Times,* in its review of *Dhalgren,* called Delany the most interesting SF writer in the English language today), the twelve-year-old can escape from the sexual frustrations of adolescence into a world of impossible sexual hospitality and freedom—and of course it is science fiction and not real, so you don't have to worry about the real world and Mommy looking over your shoulder. Ha! The reading of SF is once again an act of revolution and rebellion! The great escape is still alive and well.

The power of science fiction has changed and yet remained the same. When the SF of the last decade or so is observed from some distance, its primary revolutionary impulse seems quite obviously to have been sexual politics. The impact of this theme on the young people of the Seventies will certainly be reflected in our wider culture in the decades to come. Remember the impact of *Stranger in a Strange Land* and note that *Dhalgren,* which has sold more copies to date than Thomas Pynchon's *Gravity's Rainbow,* is now one of the most widely read SF books *outside* the SF field.

Entertainment, escape, powerful impact on the deepest levels of the human psyche flow through the conduit of SF in which the fantasies that a twelve-year-old will not allow herself in the real world suddenly confront her in clear prose on the printed page. Young women, charged with visionary energy, hang with rapt attention upon the words of Russ and Bradley and Charnas. Nowhere else in the body of contemporary literature can they experience such enchantment but in these works. Believe it, these are tales of wonder.

But these SF tales are in some ways peripheral to the concerns of the core SF audience of the early 1980s. This new generation of readers is more nearly a fantasy audience than what we have commonly identified as the SF core audience—a lot of them are young women and men who will admit to a casual dislike for science and technology. It has remained for such writers as John Varley to hold the center of the SF field in the late 1970s, to combine (as in "The Phantom of Kansas," discussed beginning on p. 97) the new thematic concerns of life-style and sexual politics with the traditional SF play of crazy ideas. Without such writers as Varley to arouse the traditional excitements of SF in the chronic audience and to satisfy the powerful needs of the new omnivores (feminists, gays, fantasy fans) who comprise an ever larger portion of the SF audience, the SF field would be in greater danger of serious fragmentation. A marked diffusion of energy is already evident through the ever larger numbers (of readers, dollars, books, everything) involved in the SF enterprise as the field escalates in the 1980s.

The promise of escape is stronger and more beguiling than ever in science fiction as writers aim for target groups within the larger overall SF field. The variety of escapes continues to proliferate.

5 | When It Comes True, It's No Fun Anymore

SPACE, space travel, the future— that's what science fiction is about. SF stories and the people who write them have always been enthusiastic about our future in space. So when Sputnik went up in 1957 and suddenly rockets to space were real, it was the greatest thing that could happen to the science fiction field. Right?

Wrong. Science is speculative (science is fiction?). When it becomes real, it's merely technology. Real space travel almost killed the science fiction field.

How? Why?

The popular idea outside the field—that somehow the business of SF is to predict what will come true—is dangerous and mistaken, a perversion of the truth of science: Science, when it works, tells you what will happen in defined circumstances every time. This is what we were all taught in school about science and what all scientists believed about science right up until the last few decades, when things like "uncertainty principles" and "wave-particle dualities" (sometimes it looks like matter and sometimes energy) began to make hard sciences like physics and chemistry look a lot more indeterminate to the scientists themselves—but more exciting and speculative, too! These days, theoretical physicists are a happy and energetic breed, with lots of really strange theories.

But until 1957, a whole lot of the creative energy of SF had gone into visions of space and space travel, producing a large majority of the popular enduring works up to that time. A wave of excitement and euphoria broke over SF in late 1957: Finally, it's real! Now everyone will know that we were right all along, all during those decades when we were called space nuts (or simply nuts)—we were the ones who had faith, who knew, and now the world is at our feet!

Within a few weeks the horrible truths began to pile up. The world didn't care that the SF field had been right all along— aside from a few early headlines and Sunday-supplement pieces about science fiction becoming science fact, no one paid any more attention to SF than they ever had. And as 1958 wore on, it got worse: Fewer and fewer people were buying and reading SF books and magazines. During the years after Sputnik, the field declined radically.

John W. Campbell, the leading spokesman for SF, came up with a rationalization typical of the elitist traditions of the SF family: Now that science fiction has proven its power to become real, people were frightened of it and stayed away. In a positively orgiastic fit of power fantasies fulfilled, Campbell asserted that the recession in SF would cleanse the field of those lily-livered readers who had never really believed in the first place, who had just come to SF for escapist adventure. Now the true elite could get on with the business of predicting other great things, such as the development of mental powers (psychic powers or "psi," and Scientology).

The truth is that in a single instant the fact of space travel turned most of the classic space travel stories of science fiction into fantasies. Every week of the new space age made more science fiction *un*true. This was such a big thing for SF that no one could quite think it through at the time. Everyone knew that something was really wrong, however, and the sudden decline in SF was a numbing disappointment to everyone, coming at the end of the great boom in SF that characterized the early Fifties.

In such classics as Heinlein's "The Man Who Sold the Moon," SF readers had been told in no uncertain terms that space travel would be a private enterprise, usually the inspiration of an Edisonlike inventor or visionary businessman. That the Russian government had gotten there first, that the U.S. military would follow in a bungling fashion (at least initially) boggled SF readers. Doc Smith's *The Skylark of Space*, Heinlein's Future History stories, all the classics and standard works were now no longer improbable but possible: They were dead wrong. Space travel, one of the greatest visions of generations of SF writers and fans, was real and the euphoria of SF fans at the fact was real, but a major and confusing readjustment was suddenly necessary.

The publication that won the Hugo Award for best amateur magazine at the 1961 World SF Convention was a fat little one-shot published in 1960 called *Who Killed Science Fiction?* The whole field knew that SF was contracting, maybe even dying on the vine, and of course everyone had his own theory of why. And wanted to fight about it. The SF magazines were contracting and some of them disappearing, and it was not apparent at the time that the new form of SF, the paperback, was stable and growing some, for magazines had been the primary source of SF since 1926, unchallenged. Fortunately science fiction was not dying, but it certainly was changing—and selling less—and for the first time since the beginning, writers and readers were actually leaving the family in significant numbers.

For years afterward, no one paid much attention to some of the other significant factors in the decline of SF in those years. Fred Pohl, among others, has repeatedly drawn attention to the simple fact that half or more of the SF publications of the Fifties were pretty marginal economically, and that in the mid-Fifties the largest magazine distributor in the U.S. was gobbled up by a conglomerate and sold off piecemeal, thus ending national distribution for about half the magazines in the U.S., including a whole lot of SF publications. Only the largest survived.

And yes, SF was changing in the Fifties—a lot of writers were trying new ways of writing. This was not necessarily what the readers wanted, and for the first time, starting at the end of the 1940s, SF began to move partially out of the controlling hands of a few knowledgeable editors and publishers into more general circulation, at the hands of powerful people who might understand the material only dimly.

From 1950 to 1954, it looked to everyone both inside and outside that science fiction was about to be recognized as major, worthwhile, meritorious—that everyone would finally stop putting science fiction down and consider it seriously on its own merits. These were the boom years. In one month during this period, forty different SF magazine titles were displayed, and could all be found on a sufficiently large newsstand; several of the prestigious hardcover publishers had begun regular hardcover SF programs, and SF also began to appear in paperback books—in fact some of the SF classics of the past began to reach general circulation through paperback publication. The first wave of science fiction movies, both profitable and popular, had been released; SF was on TV, in the daily comic strips, comic books, everywhere.

But the feast turned to sand. SF seemed to degenerate as it grew.

From *Destination Moon,* reflecting the highest aspirations of science fiction—technical accuracy, realism, romantic and exciting events—the motion picture industry learned something very important: You could make money on an ambitious SF film. But while *Destination Moon* was in production and beginning to look successful, another moviemaker decided to beat it into the marketplace with a quick, inaccurate, unrealistic SF adventure cobbled together on a low budget: *Rocketship XM.* Well, *Destination Moon* made money but *Rocketship XM* did beat it out to the theaters and made a lot of money too. So what the industry also learned was that you could make quick, cheap, inaccurate SF movies and make money.

Suddenly everyone who was doing science fiction from outside the field was using the sensational and gaudy elements of the cheapest pulp SF and ignoring any underlying seriousness. It was as if they only looked at those garish covers and never read the stuff. Popularity, it turned out, was not necessarily recognition. But at least more people than ever before were having fun with science fiction, with aliens and rocket ships and all the imagery of the field. SF was beginning to be a major repository of images for popular culture.

Which is why the initial reaction of the field to Sputnik was so overwhelmingly positive—this would show them that we had been serious all along. Instead, it showed that we had been fantastic all along—although it took several years for this to penetrate the consciousness of those in SF.

Why was this so hard for SF people to understand? The answer is that for at least twenty years before Sputnik, John W. Campbell and others had been fostering the slogan "Today's fiction—tomorrow's fact," a legacy left over from Hugo Gernsback's obsession with science education through fiction and with "true" science in stories. Campbell had been educated at M.I.T. as a nuclear physicist and was known for adding scientific explanations to manuscripts before printing them in his magazine. All evidence is that, throughout his career, Campbell believed that by using real science in stories, SF authors could predict real future events or at least real future technology, if only in the context of an adventure story. Since he was the editor of the best and most popular science fiction magazine from 1938 to the end of his life in 1971, and the most prestigious SF editor of modern times, he was most often the field's spokesman to outside groups. One of the special *frissons* was that sometimes SF really did come true and Campbell could, by the late 1940s, quote lots of examples:

H. G. Wells predicted tank warfare in "The Land Ironclads" (1903); Rudyard Kipling predicted airmail in "With the Night Mail" (1905); Hugo Gernsback made a whole forest of predictions, including that of television, in *Ralph 124C41+* (1911–12); in the early 1940s, Robert A. Heinlein ("Blowups Happen") and Lester del Rey ("Nerves") both wrote stories about the dangers of nuclear power plants; another Heinlein story, "Solution Unsatisfactory" (1941), suggests that the U.S. would be drawn into World War II, would end the war by building an atomic bomb, using the weapon to impose a "pax Americana" upon the rest of the world. In 1944, Campbell published an atom bomb story, "Deadline" by Cleve Cartmill, which contained so much accurate physics that agents of Military Intelligence descended on Campbell's office, sure of a security leak and ready to suppress the magazine. What a story for Campbell to tell after the war! And tell it he did, at every opportunity.

Dealing with the future as it might really be was portrayed by Campbell as the transcendent goal of the best science fiction, and, since he controlled the highest-paying regular market for science fiction in the world, his writers most often included a prediction or two, and the SF world waited with bated breath to see what might come true.

Robert A. Heinlein, a writer with a good engineering mind, won the prediction lottery most often. Heinlein's 1942 story "Waldo" describes a mechanical genius with a muscular disease that forces him to create a remote control device that repeats the movements of his own hands, at a distance, with equal accuracy and much greater force. When such devices were actually built a few years later to handle radioactive materials, they were named "waldoes" in honor of the story that inspired their creation.

Of course all those predictions involving atom bombs and nuclear power turned sour real quick. Science fiction people, who had been reading and writing about the atom for decades, were among the first to react with dismay. Atomic disaster stories proliferated in the late Forties and early Fifties, so the really positive and optimistic aspect of SF prediction which Campbell had to focus on was space travel. And by the early Fifties, everyone in SF, Campbell especially, knew it was just a matter of time before it would be real. There was a continual atmosphere of that triumph to come—until Sputnik.

The U.S. space program ground slowly but it ground exceeding small. Some SF people have continued to believe in the romance of space travel throughout the 1960s and 1970s, in the face of the boring facts, but a lot of others, particularly sensitive to what had been their own province for decades, became more and more alienated from U.S. media/government space travel. What good is it to have predicted all of this technology, from space suits and orbital velocities to stage rockets and communi-

cation satellites, if roles can be performed by trained chimpan-
zees? Where is the vision and romance and excitement?

Well, to some the excitement remained—there is a certain
charm and beauty in machines that perform well and are, after
all, built and created by humans. But the heroic astronauts
began to retire and become politicians(!) and administrators(!)
and converts to religious sects(!). By the time of the second
moon landing, all according to TV script and utterly anticlimac-
tic, even the most committed SF people had begun to mutter
and grumble that the right thing was being done by the wrong
people in the wrong way. How could they make it so unroman-
tic? How could they!

When science fiction comes true, it's no fun anymore. Even
Campbell recognized, as early as 1950, with the advent of
Galaxy and the *Magazine of Fantasy and Science Fiction,*
major new magazines with editorial policies radically different
from Campbell's, that his idea of science fiction's qualities had
some serious competition even within the field.

All during the 1940s, while *Astounding* was supreme, a
bunch of other magazines—pulps such as *Startling Stories,
Planet Stories,* and *Thrilling Wonder Stories*—were publishing
fantastic SF that made little pretense at scientific accuracy but
still gripped the readers. Such upstart writers as Ray Bradbury,
Leigh Brackett, Jack Vance, Frederic Brown, John D. MacDonald rarely if ever sold to Campbell—not enough science in their
fiction, for the most part—science fantasy writers mostly, not in
the mainstream of SF. None of their stuff could ever happen.

Well, it turns out from the vantage point of hindsight that
except for a very few instances, no one ever actually set out
primarily to predict through science fiction. H. G. Wells did,
sometimes, in his later works. Perhaps Heinlein did, sometimes,
but always subordinate to telling a good story. Certainly Gernsback did. But don't get the idea that very many SF readers and
writers ever accepted Campbell's argument—it seems to have
been much more widespread, a cliché even, outside the field.
Meanwhile the cliché, the joke, was that with all the SF being
published, it stands to reason that someone, somewhere, will be
at least partly right once in a while and predict something—but

more by luck than intent. SF writers have never intended to be prophets, nor have most readers expected it of them.

The dominance of heavily science-oriented SF was broken by the advent of the new markets of the Fifties, by new editors such as H. L. Gold (*Galaxy*) who was particularly interested in varieties of social and political extrapolation rather than technological extrapolation, and by Anthony Boucher, editor of the *Magazine of Fantasy and Science Fiction,* who was interested in fantasy and SF and in stylistic excellence, in equal parts. New writers rose to prominence—Ray Bradbury, Frederik Pohl, William Tenn, Theodore Sturgeon, Robert Sheckley, Arthur C. Clarke, Alfred Bester, Damon Knight, James Blish, Clifford D. Simak, and a host of others—to join the Campbellian pantheon of Heinlein, Asimov, Van Vogt and L. Ron Hubbard. This was the era from which come most of the acknowledged classics of contemporary SF.

What these authors and their peers do is better than prediction—they envision, then analyze their visions to show how they work. They are in the habit of creating a science fictional world that may indeed be highly improbable for a "real" future, but then they focus sincere concentration on the way that envisioned world could work, especially certain selected aspects of it.

The aspects a writer selects often characterize that writer to the SF community. Hal Clement is known for his creation of astrophysically interesting worlds in space as settings for his SF adventures. Larry Niven is known for carrying on Clement's tradition and for creating interesting alien races and technological artifacts. Theodore Sturgeon is known for using SF settings for investigating complex human behavior and psychology. Arthur C. Clarke is known for portraying technology and environment in space. The list could go on, but the examples all tell us how things work. Readers escape into these visions because they are able to suspend disbelief and participate in the exciting process of having the vision's works revealed.

And neither the reader nor the writer is expected to believe in the vision itself, necessarily—it might be just a wonderful, unlikely hypothesis. Look at the small type on the back of the title page in any edition of Arthur C. Clarke's great SF novel

Childhood's End and you will find this note: "The opinions expressed in this book are not those of the author." Not only is *Childhood's End* just a science fictional vision, it is also a vision that contradicts what the writer believes to be the true and real. But while we, and Clarke, are caught up in the vision, we are convinced that this is how it would or should work. The vision of *Childhood's End* is metaphysical in the tradition of Olaf Stapledon—while humanity transcends science and technology in the end, Clarke doesn't believe that we should or could—but his personal beliefs are external to the novel. Many readers of SF prefer Clarke's metaphysical to his more technological visions of the future.

The basic rule of thumb in the SF community for critical discussion has always been "It works/it doesn't work." A couple of years back, Samuel R. Delany appeared before a group of seniors at Stevens Institute of Technology who were taking an elective in science fiction. One of them asked him to explain a bothersome point regarding a minor classic by Bob Shaw, "Light of Other Days," in which the idea of "slow glass" is envisioned ("slow glass" is glass through which light takes so long to pass that you can see the past through it as if it were now). The student had done calculations and found that slow glass could not work the way Shaw declared it would in the story. Doesn't this invalidate the story, Mr. Delany? No, said Delany, the point is that the explanation has to be untrue or the story would be present technology, not future science—Shaw's explanation is credible and intelligent but is still a lie told for the greater good of the *idea*.

Shaw may or may not point in the right direction with his explanation, but SF operates in a universe where things are explainable, so Shaw creates an explanation, which is false, for his visionary idea, which is authentic, so that the idea does not seem to violate what is known *when explained*. Delany told the student that if he could do more calculations and find out how slow glass would really work, then he could make it, but Shaw's vision remains valid anyway, even after reality contradicts it, because truth according to the rules of present science is not the business of science fiction. And SF specifically is concerned with possibility that does not offend against what is known to be known.

When an idea from SF does come true, it may be gratifying for a short while, but it is the pleasure of serendipitous discovery, ironic. *Camp Concentration* (1968), a novel by Thomas M. Disch, concerns a U.S. government prison facility wherein the prisoners are intentionally given a syphilislike spirochete as an experiment to see if their intelligence is increased before they die. Several years after the novel was published, it was revealed in the *New York Times* that government researchers had indeed carried on a similar research program: a wrongheaded 1930s medical experiment in which certain cases of syphilis were allowed to go untreated—to which news Disch responded with irony, "I was right!" He had predicted the past!

SF authors are prophets of wonder. Specifics are not the point. Prophets speak in images that must be interpreted, not in literal statements. SF ideas have "come true," but never in precisely the manner of the story wherein they originate. Waldoes were not in fact invented to help an eccentric, brilliant victim of myasthenia gravis manipulate his environment, but to manage radioactive materials safely at a distance. Yet the public wants prophecy and they want it literal—What *will* happen next? There has been enormous public pressure on SF and on SF writers, since the first of its "predictions" that turned out to be true, to be oracular, to create microwave ovens and better Saranwrap and to predict the next war. No wonder it's no fun when it comes true. It's so often minor league.

Still, the visionary enterprise remains wonderful for SF author and audience. And some SF authors, such as Frederik Pohl (an active futurologist), engage in activities peripheral to SF, such as corporate think tank sessions or futurology conferences, which try to bring the visionary aspects of SF into predictive use. Various think tanks (whose purposes include developing practical solutions to anticipated future problems so that the future can be directed) sometimes use SF that bears upon the problem at hand as a repository of solutions or to develop a catalogue of far-out possibilities. The futurologists, whose purposes include describing near-future probabilities so that we as individuals can prepare appropriate responses and not be incapacitated by future shock, also use SF as a mental exercise in considering possibilities.

Everyone feels that SF should be *used* and that prophecy is somehow the most appropriate use. It is truly extraordinary, when you think about it, that a form of literature published for entertainment should have such public pressure brought to bear on its utility. And it makes some SF writers, every once in a while, really want what they write to come true. This has caused some repercussions in the real world.

The author of the famous *Riverworld* novels, Philip Jose Farmer, wrote a Hugo award-winning story in the mid-Sixties, "Riders of the Purple Wage," about a revolutionary new economic system. He then suggested to the membership of the World Science Fiction Convention in 1968, in a legendary guest of honor speech, that the SF world band together to put this system into action. Hardly anyone took him seriously, a deep disappointment. But consider the story of L. Ron Hubbard.

Hubbard was a flamboyant pulp SF writer for Campbell's *Astounding* in the late Thirties and throughout the Forties. He wrote on a continuous roll of paper, wore cowboy boots, and filled the room with his presence. He had big ideas. In 1949 he wrote a speculative nonfiction essay published in 1950 in *Astounding* announcing his development of Dianetics, "the modern science of mental health." His ideas were immediately taken seriously, published at book length and won thousands of converts; they even became a source of controversy in the letter column of the *New York Times*. Dianetics in subsequent years took on the name Scientology and became a "scientific" religion.

Scientology was originally a psychological training system through which you could become so wonderfully sane that you could attain wonders of physical and psychological control over yourself and your environment, ridding yourself of pernicious engrams (prenatal influences). Its unusual history and development is littered with scandals and public controversies. In the last decade it was revealed that the Scientologists had infiltrated the F.B.I.! Recently, the question of whether L. Ron Hubbard is alive or dead (one of his heirs forced him to prove himself alive) made national news. Whatever the inside story of Scientology is, it has never been told thoroughly—but it is clear that the cult is a significant force and Hubbard a powerful and mysterious figure today.

What excites people outside SF is when you claim that what you are saying is literally true (e.g., flying saucers are real). And many people within the SF community, because of Hubbard's standing in the field and because Campbell himself was a convert (Campbell maintained throughout his life that he believed in the techniques of Dianetics), took up the "new science." After all, the result of participating in the new science was to be that through training and hard work, you would become saner than everybody else (that familiar elitist strain). Hubbard left SF immediately to devote full time to his new science and took with him A. E. Van Vogt (author of *Slan*), then at the height of his reputation as one of the top four or five SF writers, and a number of lesser lights. Van Vogt returned to writing SF in the late Sixties, but Hubbard still lives the life of a wealthy cult leader on his yacht. His ideas have come true, so to speak. He is no longer primarily a writer but a prophet.

Even so, a huge new SF novel by Hubbard appeared in 1983 and made the national best-seller lists, buoyed up by a large publicity campaign. We are promised an even larger opus, over a million words, in 1985. Hubbard was always a writer to contend with in the Thirties and Forties and now, with the power of his church behind him, his sudden comeback is sure to be interesting. Perhaps we have a prophet turning into a writer again.

SF readers want SF authors to be prophets, but not in the Hubbard manner or in the restricted sense of predictors. After all, an SF story about a new kind of liquid fuel for a NASA rocket would probably be uninteresting and perhaps unpublishable, no matter how accurate. The idea just isn't very big and exciting. What SF readers want is for writers to come up with projections, not of the most likely, but of the most interesting and original futures. They want, in other words, prophetic images. And SF today is faced with a time problem, as we remarked earlier, since the newly investigated solar system has made fantasy out of many of its classics. As a result, there is a great rise in the popularity of fantasy and science fantasy, while the whole SF field strives to come up with new settings that have the range, power, and immediacy of the interplanetary future of our recent past.

In the interim, while the outright fantasy genre invades the SF market, perhaps the most successful mass market magazine founded in a decade is *Omni,* an odd mixture of science, SF, psychic phenomena, and flying saucers, which came out of left field (the successful publisher of one of the hairy competitors of *Playboy*) to sell a million copies per issue. One can see the immediate appeal of *Omni* in its vivid and lovely graphics, but the editorial appeal is comprehensible only if one understands that the public's desire for prophetic images is strong today, and *Omni* presents a variety of these images in a format that is not cheap but rather is classy and respectable. Somehow *Omni* taps a search for truth through these images. If it continues to succeed, it will do so because it continues to hold out the promise of revelation. This promise is basically the same that SF holds out to its readers. The difference is that SF fulfills the promise in giving wonderful images, while *Omni* can only promise to search for truth, and publish a little SF.

Prophesy is tricky business and most SF writers would back-step quickly away and into the nearest bar for fortification if you told any one of them he was a prophet. Nevertheless, SF is a wellspring of prophecy, its writers are prophets not by high calling and appointment but simply by doing the job of writing SF well, by envisioning a future and showing how it works (or how it doesn't), how it interacts with human nature. We need only look at the examples of famous SF novels over the last century or so that have leaned toward social prophecy to verify that it is not the prediction but the prophetic vision wherein the power resides.

Consider for a moment that Nikolay Chernyshevsky's *What Is to Be Done?*, certainly a catalyst of the events in Russia that culminated in the 1917 revolution, is essentially an SF novel. In the U.S., we have the interesting case of Colonel House, Woodrow Wilson's closest adviser, who published in 1912 an SF novel called *Philip Dru: Administrator*, predicting civil war in the U.S. in the 1920s and 1930s. At the height of his power during the Wilson administration, House, according to historian

Christopher Lasch, "found it increasingly difficult to distinguish what was happening from what he had predicted was to happen." Then, of course, we have Huxley's *Brave New World* and Orwell's *1984*, such dominant images of prophecy in our culture that the very titles have come to stand for specific potential realities. Finally there is the whole area of utopian and dystopian fiction, which early in this century became almost entirely conflated with science fiction (in previous centuries, utopias were often set in the present; now, with rare exceptions such as Skinner's *Walden Two*, they are set in the future)—most of our social visions in the latter half of this century are SF.

Sometimes, for better or worse, the imagery of SF is so strong that someone caught by it decides to act out some SF in the real world. Stephen Gaskin, spiritual and temporal leader of the largest and most successful rural commune, the Farm in Summertown, Tennessee, author of *Monday Night Class* and other books, read a great deal of SF when he was young and acknowledges that it gave him ideas, such as how people might be telepathic with one another, that he has gone on to act out. Jane Roberts, the medium through which the spirit "Seth" communicates to us mortals (she is listed as the author of the books) was for many years an active SF writer who held a famous séance in the 1950s involving Damon Knight, A. J. Budrys, and Cyril Kornbluth among others. But there is very little science in the real-life fictions of Roberts and Gaskin, and of Charles Manson, mentioned earlier, and SF pales into a minor shadow in light of their other accomplishments, metaphysical, criminal, or social.

More significant and more complex is the decades-long desire on the part of a large number of otherwise average people to interact with flying saucers. This is turning SF images into reality with a vengeance.

Have you ever read one of the hundreds of books about flying saucers? If so, you will remember that most of the wordage is spent trying to tell you in one way or another that "they're real." The question of why it should be so important to so many people for flying saucers to be real or true has seldom been addressed (but was, notably, by C. G. Jung in his book on the subject), and certainly not in most of the pro-saucer literature. Few publishers are foolish enough to publish anti-saucer material—no one cares to buy it. The gist of the matter seems to be that flying saucers are messengers and the message is not knowledge but transcendence.

Only recently has the situation calmed down for people in the SF community, most especially for the writers—for from the late 1940s to the 1970s, the most common questions asked by an outsider of a science fiction person was "Do you believe in flying saucers? What do you think of them?" The immediate assumption was that anyone in SF would know more than the ordinary person about things such as flying saucers; so for more than a decade SF was known in some circles as "that flying saucer stuff"—a perversion of the fairly accurate "that space stuff." All this happened initially without any cooperation from the SF community at all—except that flying saucers did in fact begin to appear from time to time in SF stories up to and including *Star Trek* (note that the main body of the *Enterprise* is a saucer). SF had spent many years prophesying visitors from space and the image stuck in the popular consciousness in a manner no one from Wells on down could have predicted. Early signs of it were evident in the reaction to the famous Halloween broadcast of *The War of the Worlds*, when thousands panicked because they *believed* in it.

When it comes true it can be dangerous and frightening.

And it is fairly evident that thousands, if not more, are acting out SF fantasies in the real world now and today, because they believe in psi powers or invading aliens or whatever. Let us hope that the fantasies are benign.

Because SF deals with big ideas, the images SF authors use are often powerful and large, commensurate with the breadth of vision in a given work. Sometimes the power springs from the uncanniness of the alien, but more often it arises from playing with huge-scale distances, immense scope, great size—larger than life. Visions of galactic civilizations, mind-boggling technology, eons of time are supposed to distance us from the mundane here-and-now. But aside from these absolute clichés, which need no explanation, the big images are supposed to be rationalized, explaining how and why things work the way they do in the world of the story, as Bob Shaw did for his "slow glass." If you don't get the idea that the explanations are essentially a convention to establish verisimilitude, using contemporary science as a springboard, and if you believe after the story is over that what you read is in some way literally real, then you are in deep trouble and should perhaps join the Baker Street Irregulars (who purport to believe in Sherlock Holmes). It is much safer for the rest of us. I am not, after all, here to recommend expensive therapy, and we all should have a rich fantasy life, if nothing else.

On the other hand, it is okay if you happen to be a scientist or engineer and happen to have some free time and want to play around with how something like that device you just read about might actually work and be constructed. You just might, then, invent it, as Frederik Pohl does in *The Gold at the Starbow's End* (New York: Ballantine, 1972, p. 46):

> *Most problems have grammatical solutions.* The problem of transporting people from the Earth to another planet does not get solved by putting pieces of steel together one at a time at random and happening to find out you've built the [spaceship] by accident. It gets solved by constructing a model (=equation (=grammar) which describes the necessary circumstances under which the transportation occurs. Once you have the grammatical model, you just put the metal around it and it goes like gangbusters.

You would then have created a prediction, which, until that moment, would only have been one speculative idea among many. The author would necessarily have fantasized in his "grammatical model" and your achievement would be to modify, revise, and correct it until it becomes scientifically and technologically accurate.

Today's fiction, tomorrow's fact!

That SF stories are in some sense possible is essential to the pleasure of SF as opposed to fantasy. That every once in a while a speculation turns into a prediction because someone up and invents the space suit or the waldo or some such in real life provides concrete verification of SF as "possible" fiction. It *is* fun, in this one particular sense, when it comes true, because in a special way it validates the whole developing literary aesthetic of SF (the best book on the subject to date is Samuel R. Delany's *Starboard Wine,* 1984). But it doesn't have to happen very often, and coming true, as we have seen, is not really the point.

To make it the point is to rob the vast majority of SF of its validity as vision. And to believe in the "fun lies" of SF without questioning them in the real world is dumb and, at worst, could lead to a life of crime.

Please, don't believe it for a moment. It's all in fun.

6 Where Do You Get Those Crazy Ideas?

"**WHERE** do your ideas come from?" That question so often asked of science fiction writers by neo-fans, the media, relatives who don't read SF, and all manner of outsiders was answered once, tongue in cheek, by SF author Roger Zelazny. In front of a group of fans at a convention, he replied to a vacuous teenager that the *Journal of Crazy Ideas* is published quarterly in Schenectady, New York, and that when you join the Science Fiction Writers of America and become a certified professional you get a free subscription and can use any of the ideas in the magazine instead of having to think up your own. This is one of the secrets of being a professional and one of the reasons why two different writers will have the same idea in different stories.

The reason the question is difficult to answer is that there are so many true answers. Asimov, you will remember, got the idea for "Nightfall" from John W. Campbell—until the end of the 1950s it was common for SF writers to get story ideas directly from an editor such as Campbell or *Galaxy*'s Horace Gold. It was also standard practice from the early 1930s to the beginning of the 1970s for a writer to be given the cover story of a magazine, by which we mean that the editor of a pulp would buy a piece of commercial illustration from an artist for use on the cover, fitting the image and marketing approach of the magazine, and then call in one or more writers and assign them the job of writing a story to fit and tie into the cover illustration. Alfred Bester, for instance, wrote his extraordinary story "5,271,009" for the *Magazine of Fantasy and Science Fiction* on assignment to fit a painting of a man in old-fashioned prison stripes and glass space helmet sitting alone on a boulder-sized piece of rock in space. The number on his prison suit is 5,271,009. Bester's story is about the number (used as a leitmotif). In the commercial field of magazine writing (originally the pulp field) you were often assigned ideas.

Another true answer is that ideas are everywhere and they occur to you, the writer, all the time. Except when they don't, and then you wait until they do. This is not a satisfactory answer because it is so universally true; and besides, anyone who asks such a question is sure that you have a secret to tell them and won't be satisfied with general truth. Which is why science fiction writers, just like all other artists, lie a lot. You can't just say that every idea is individual, a unique case. Or, worst of all, that really most SF ideas are lifted and altered consciously or unconsciously from other SF stories and that this is an honorable tradition in the field. But this is perhaps the most meaningful answer. We will explore it in detail in a few moments.

First, though, let's consider the plight of the science fiction writer who wants to use an idea. Initially, she must ask herself the same question that most teenagers are unable to answer in, say, math class when confronted with the square root of minus one: How can this mean anything in reality? Can I conceive of a situation in which this abstract idea would be of relevant and crucial significance in the life of a human being or humanity? In the days of Hugo Gernsback, this really meant to a writer "Can I use this idea to build a machine that will do something?" But it has come to mean what Ursula K. Le Guin has described for us in chapter 2, something that reverberates with thematic implications.

Yet I want to make a distinction between the central and overarching ideas of science fiction, of individual works even, and the more general and stimulating free flow of supporting ideas and bits of information combined and recombined in story after story. The kind of overwhelming flow of input to the reader that has led Theodore Sturgeon to define SF as "knowledge fiction." SF writers tend to be magpies for odd facts and bits of knowledge of all sorts. Alfred Bester has told in his speeches and essays how he has always kept a notebook of interesting facts and events, which he then puts in his stories, suitably adapted. Science fiction readers desire these ideas as part of the environment of the fiction, admire a story that is full of ideas of all sorts, historical, theological, technological, psychological, you name it. As long as the story integrates the ideas into the fiction and makes them concrete—or creates a fictional situation wherein ideas are discussed seriously, especially from several points of view or a new point of view—it's acceptable SF.

The net effect of all these ideas is to alienate most uninitiated readers. We have heard too many people say for too many years that science fiction is just too fantastic for the average person of taste. At the same time we see that the books and shows these people do like are filled with illogical and preposterous coincidences and monstrous and mechanical oversimplifications of human psychology from Harold Robbins and Judith Krantz to *I Love Lucy* and such mass market phenomena as Silhouette Romance. They want an incredible (to SF people) sense of ordinariness in the details surrounding whatever fantasy they read—and make no mistake, they are reading nothing but fantasies—as if their imaginations have been brutally trained to function only in an environment of endless and boring repetition. The only things that are real to them are things they have seen before. It sure feeds the ego of SF people to feel superior to all these others—who may in daily life be more canny and sharp and successful than SF people have ever been.

If you don't particularly want your consciousness raised about certain subjects, any subjects, then reading a fair amount of science fiction can be threatening. Because sooner rather than later, you are going to run into a science fiction story that adopts an a priori world view different from yours. After all, one of the absolute givens of the whole of SF is that every single story must take place in a world that is not, in some identifiable manner, mundane reality. As a body of literature, science fiction is a catalogue or encyclopedia of ideas about how things might be, might have been, or really are—although we don't know it yet.

The most comfortable and nonthreatening kind of science fiction would seem to be the stuff set 3,000,000 years in the future on a distant planet, nicely distanced from anything real and nearby. Many SF readers prefer this type of SF, usually cast as space opera, with good guys and villains, ray guns and spaceships, and the odd alien or three. It can be wonderful escape. But even in this kind of paraphernalia-filled adventure, you are being asked to believe, for a moment, in an adventurous, optimistic future filled with technological wonders and exceeding strangeness. And if you do limit your reading to only this kind of stuff, and even one minor element of it comes true right here today—like spaceships suddenly translating from the realm of space adventure into the NASA program, then you are threatened, you have to rethink a basic preconception and consider, for at least a millisecond, the possibility of rethinking others. In a minority of cases, you are then further hooked on SF—otherwise you stop reading it and turn to other areas for escape from the humdrum.

The committed SF reader gets part of his excitement from knowing that every new story will require some reconsideration of reality. Some idea, some new bit of information or speculation or recombination of old ideas will require thought, excite the mind as well as the viscera.

And, for goodness sake, some of the ideas are there for the pure fun of it. Not for contemplation or significance, or even to help validate the setting—some ideas are included by some writers just for atmosphere, for the sake of humor, or better, wit. The short stories of William Tenn or Robert Sheckley or Ron Goulart, Bester's novels, much of Frederik Pohl's short fiction are all examples of playful ideas supporting serious purpose.

Add all of the foregoing up, and science fiction is jam-packed with ideas of all sorts. Some chronics maintain that they read SF for the ideas alone, from the definitely possible to the widely improbable. In *Future Shock,* Alvin Toffler recommended that SF be studied and read by adults and taught to children to insulate them, through exposure to the vast interplay of possibilities, from a feeling of defeat in the face of unceasing change. Science fiction reading, he said, protects you against future shock, instills right thinking, makes you ready to adapt to change because it teaches you to assume change as inevitable. This is true, certainly, and is another way in which science fiction can be used, just as it can be used to teach religion. But the primary purpose of all those ideas is to entertain: to allow you, for a moment, to consider the idea in passing and draw whatever pleasure you can from it. And part of the game is the free access of all the other writers in the field to your ideas and yours to theirs. T. S. Eliot, the author of "Tradition and the Individual Talent," who said that good poets borrow and great poets steal, would have approved.

I would like to take you on a trip through a very good science fiction story, in all its complication, and show you ideas in place. The story is "The Phantom of Kansas" by John Varley, an early work of this popular young author which was first published in 1976 in *Galaxy* and later collected in *The Persistence of Vision,* one of the most important science fiction books of the last decade. Varley's story is a particularly successful tale of wonder and allows us to examine in some detail the role played by a proliferation of ideas within a science fiction story both in supporting the development of the central thematic complex and in creating independent flashes of wonder, moments of intellectual excitement and gooseflesh as the story progresses.

"I do my banking at the Archimedes Trust Association." The first sentence of the story introduces the first-person narrator and indicates, by use of the present tense, that the speaker assumes a contemporary audience. This is a common device in science fiction—an experienced reader of science fiction knows the several signals this technique conveys: that contemporary to the speaker does *not* mean contemporary to the reader and that the "when" of the story will emerge from the narrative through significant details; further, that Archimedes is a famous location on the moon, so that the matter-of-fact tone and the focus on the ordinary detail of banking suggest the possibility of a large and significant disparity between our world and the world of the story. This possibility is immediately confirmed in the second sentence, which indicates that the bank has its own "medico facility" and "takes recordings for the vaults." This must be a new and different kind of bank—the reader's anticipation is whetted, knowing that a new idea is about to be unveiled. But first a narrative hook—the plot is introduced: The bank was robbed two weeks ago.

Then, pow! The next two paragraphs contain in summary the caper plot for a whole mystery and detective novel. In this world, the technological re-creation of personality is possible, using recordings made regularly (to insure that your policy is up to date) and stored in bank vaults in plastic memory cubes, along with valuables and "negotiable paper." When a bank robbery occurs, it is most often only a blind for the destruction of the memory cubes, since you can't murder someone who has been recorded—he won't stay dead unless you destroy the cube—and you destroy lots of cubes so the police won't know whom you are going to kill. But this is all by the way. As a result of the robbery, the narrator is about to be rerecorded quickly, at the bank's expense—"They had contracted to keep me alive forever." Of course! This technology really means immortality! And this implication is just slid in as part of the everyday world of the story, never mentioned again—a wonderful moment.

The eighth paragraph of the story makes it clear that all of this is passing through the narrator's mind in the moments before the narrator is led into the recording room. We are not fully in the dramatic present of the story: As the narrator is prepared for recording, there is a moment of reflection on having lived so long and met so many people over so many decades. How old *is* the narrator? We never really know, since this is a world in which it literally does not matter. As the narrator passes into unconsciousness for recording, we are left for a moment with this new idea to ponder.

As the narrator awakens, one of the attendants says, "She's in," and we know for the first time that the narrator is female. And though the narrative persona is continuous, she finds that she has died and been reborn in a new body two and a half years later—two pages later, she learns that she has died three times in those years, that she is the fourth incarnation of herself: "We suspect murder," says the bank president.

The heroine's multiple deaths are used to ignite the big idea of the story: the problems and complexity of preserving personal identity in this particular future ("the first order of business was to recognize that the things that were done by those three previous people were not done by *me*."). Two years and more have been lost from her life, in which she lived and died, but which she can never remember because "she," the first-person narrator, wasn't there—she is discontinuous. (The person who wakes up is a print of the recording made two and a half years ago—so she can have only the memories that belonged to her when she was recorded. She knows nothing of what "she" did after the recording was made.) She learns the circumstances of her three deaths and, it seems, we have a murder mystery on our hands.

Then a whole new thread is introduced. We learn that Fox, the narrator, is an artist in a new art form: weather. This is the moon, after all, where only artificial weather can exist. And we get another infusion of ideas.

> I had been robbed of an entire symphony. For the last thirty years I had been an Environmentalist. I had just drifted into it while it was still an infant art form. I had been in charge of the weather machines at the Transvaal disneyland, which was new at the time and the biggest and most modern of all the environmental parks in Luna. A few of us had started tinkering with the weather programs. . . . Later we invited friends to watch the storms and sunsets we concocted. . . . At the time of my last recording I had been one of the top three Environmentalists on Luna.

What a rich idea complex, a wonderful layering and mixing of inventions, analogies, and extrapolations! Environmental parks called "disneylands" on the moon, weather machines, the evolution of an art form. And then Fox 1 (the first of her three murdered selves) "went on to compose *Liquid Ice* . . . the high point of the art to date." But she, Fox 4, has no memory of the creative process or the accomplishment of *Liquid Ice,* so her work has been stolen from her. Her whole identity is in question. In a single page of text we have a new art form, with all attendant paraphernalia—performances, reviews, cash rewards, and the intangible rewards of creativity (these last stolen from her)—and in the further course of the story, one pleasure for the reader is the revelation of more of the details of this art form, in which the artist works in tandem with a benign computer (the great "CC," central computer, which runs the whole civilization) to create a program for the weather machines.

A forest of further complications arises as the plot progresses, as Isadora, the detective, outlines the problems and complexities of finding a criminal in this future society—knowing that the killer was a man when he killed Fox 3 tells them nothing, for he could have bought a "Change" the next day. Even an individual's sex is technologically alterable at whim, for a price. Here is a society where identity is truly complex in every way.

Our narrator meditates on the problems of immortality and identity: Thousands of years in the future, there will live a being who is at least partly her, still "stringing chunks of experience onto her life" but with all her memories, even remembering her first sex change. So the loss of crucial memories, such as the creation of *Liquid Ice,* is the worst kind of disaster. "Robbed! Violated!" she exclaims dramatically to herself. And we become sentimentally involved in her desire to triumph over this foul murderer (even though Varley does overdo it by a hair).

Time passes and Fox must stay locked in her apartment while Isadora uses the police computers to attempt to track the killer down. Fox is content, for she is creating her next great work, *A Conflagration of Cyclones,* to be performed in the Kansas disneyland (note the allusion to *Oz*). CC, the benign computer with "free will" (borrowed, I think, from Samuel R. Delany's *Empire Star*), becomes an important supporting character. We learn details of the planned artwork, absorb information about the world of the future, a fascinating environment—and find that Fox inhabits an attractive seventeen-year-old forced-grown clone body (the body has had its development speeded up). The benign computer is a marvelously effective expository device, especially since it can suggest information: Perhaps the murderer was a "ghost." "The term 'ghost' covers all illegal beings. . . . These are executed criminals with their right to life officially revoked, unauthorized children never registered, and some suspected artificial mutants. . . . They have no right to life. I must execute them when I find them. . . . It's a job humans find distasteful. I never could keep the position filled, so I assumed it myself."

By this point in the story the chronic reader of science fiction will have spotted enough allusions in this story to know that it takes place in the same future landscape as a number of Varley's other stories, a future where sex and body design changes are the accepted norm, when humanity has adapted itself to live on most of the planets and moons of the solar system, but no longer on Old Earth, from which the race has been exiled by unknowable and superior alien beings (not present in this story). This allusive technique is a borrowing from Robert A. Heinlein's famous Future History series (in turn a borrowing from H. G. Wells's *When the Sleeper Wakes*). The chronic reader derives an additional dimension of pleasure from perceiving a wider context for the events. But the unnoticed allusions all function in place for the uninitiated reader as simply additional details increasing the verisimilitude of the context.

But return to our catalogue of the ideas of the story. Identity is confirmed in this society by analysis from a tiny skin sample of the unique genetic pattern of the individual—such samples are used in place of ID cards and credit cards—and this technique is infallible. If the killer is a ghost and is captured, he will be killed.

The night of the performance of *A Conflagration of Cyclones* arrives and Fox goes to Kansas to witness her opening. We are treated to a vivid description of the show. At the climax of the performance, it becomes evident to Fox that someone is tampering with it: her killer. She finds him, confronts him, and discovers that he is her!—of course, a ghost, a phantom of herself.

She cannot bring herself to kill her double. They talk and we discover that he was created by the initial bank robbers by error, and set free by them to be caught and destroyed. Instead, to survive, he killed her, desperately, three times—but he cannot do it again. They make love in the weather, and she decides that they must be together, he must be saved.

She develops a careful plan to save him by emigrating to Pluto (a frontier planet where his existence is not illegal) and succeeds in buying her own spaceship and getting him aboard. The romantic denouement occurs in a final scene in which the CC clears them for takeoff and reveals that it is aware of what is happening, yet is allowing it to happen. Working closely with Fox and her art has given this cold machine a sense of mercy. Humanity and its technology triumphs.

Whew! We remind you that all this has taken place in a long short story, not a novel, and that "The Phantom of Kansas" is the work of a talented newcomer, not a mature and experienced artist. Nevertheless, it is a highly developed example of the science fiction story, a particularly satisfying reading experience for most segments of the SF audience. Even readers who find the romantic subplot corny or unconvincing are delighted by the steady flow of original and stimulating ideas.

The big idea of the story is the changes that may be wrought on human identity by what we might term the technology of identity—sex change, cosmetic surgery, cloning, transfer of memory by technological means—and what complex, subtle new problems and variations could result from this technology. We even have a new kind of illegal love. The crazy ideas that fill the story—weather art, memory banks, disneylands, ghosts, and the digressions on art and the critics, police procedure, history, alien invaders—all make the story better and more popular science fiction. Every one of those crazy ideas contributes specifically to the wonderful world of the story, a world that reveals itself to the reader only through the details of these ideas.

As near as we can pinpoint it, without becoming absurdly categorical, the stimulation of sense of wonder by Varley arises not just from the big idea of the story or from the crazy ideas, but from the whole story situation, from the big idea in the context of the crazy ideas. Not all big ideas evoke wonder, nor all crazy ideas—but both can and will when set within a well-told story.

We are reading and discussing stories such as the Varley piece in a more concentrated and analytic fashion than you would under normal circumstances, when you might not even notice many of the details in the pleasurable heat of reading. The point is that there are a whole lot of ideas, major and minor, borrowed and new, all organized and in place in the story. Some, if not all, of the ideas have an impact on you, the reader, even if you are skimming the story on a bus, snacking on science fiction.

The crazy ideas of science fiction are not always really serious (such as the idea of space travel) and thematically complex (such as Varley's personality recording and the problem of identity). Something like the famous "eggplant that ate Chicago" is the *reductio ad absurdum* crazy idea. But in a real SF story (as opposed to a media representation) the craziness is ordered and placed within the self-defined boundaries of the story so that it is specifically not absurd, however improbable: Absurdity is produced by taking the idea out of context. "The Phantom of Kansas" is a story about a future in which a woman is killed three times by a duplicate of herself. The duplicate is a man, and on the fourth try they get a chance to talk, fall in love, and leave the country to live together as a perfect couple.

That sort of summary is the other side of the question we discussed in chapter 3, in this case a summary without the essentials of context which make a story rational and encourage suspension of disbelief. Misrepresentation of SF as absurdity is the most common response of an uninitiated reader to the ideas in SF. SF people are so used to this kind of treatment that they often do it ironically.

It is a thin line sometimes between irony and absurdity. People in SF have always treasured such works as the vignettes of Frederic Brown (and his novel *What Mad Universe*), the stories of William Tenn, Robert Sheckley, Ron Goulart, Spider Robinson's Callahan's Saloon stories, Arthur C. Clarke's *Tales from the White Hart,* and Henry Kuttner's stories of Gallagher, the drunken inventor. Often in these stories, the purpose is to take an absurdity and place it in a story situation, the stranger the better, that allows it to be science fiction and therefore no longer (ironically) an absurdity.

In Kuttner's "The Proud Robot," Gallagher builds an enormously complicated robot while drunk, then cannot figure out its purpose when he sobers up—the robot just hangs around admiring itself while Gallagher tries to solve an involved problem concerning the future of the television industry. At the end, it is discovered that the robot is a beer can opener and, secondarily, can solve the TV problem. In the last line of the story, Gallagher is singing a duet with his can opener. Kuttner's story, written in 1942, is as full of surprising and strange ideas as the Varley story. It projects a future world in which television is the dominant form of entertainment for the middle class, when average people drink beer in front of the TV instead of going to theaters, when robots are real and domestic beer is sold in plastic containers. But there is no doubt that the serious extrapolation is the background and the craziest ideas the foreground of "The Proud Robot." It is supposed to be funny— the world turned upside down.

Sometimes, as in the stories of Tenn, Pohl, Dick, and John Sladek, it is difficult for an outsider to penetrate the deadpan surface to appreciate the often complex ironies that the crazy ideas produce. And a New Wave story such as Michael Moorcock's "The Pleasure Garden of Felipe Sagittarius" is all wit, irony, and absurdity, without a visibly developed SF context to encompass it in (proving to any outsider who gets hold of it that everything I have said above is not universally true).

I have used "crazy" to characterize the ideas of which SF is a repository. It is about time that we examined "crazy" a bit more closely. We understand that it is a term of casual derogation used for decades by outsiders to apply to all SF ideas (all the ideas used in SF stories that were not in fact true). But I have been using the term in a somewhat more specialized manner, applying it either to the complex of ideas in a given SF story which surrounds the central or big idea, or to the general play of ideas (or playing with ideas) that occurs in an SF story.

Not all of these ideas are worthwhile or intelligent, of course. Many of the minor background or supporting ideas in SF are glib fabrications included to justify logical inconsistencies created by or necessary to the central idea of the story. And a lot of the ideas in SF are stuck in there in spite of the fact that they really have nothing to do with the story: digressions that interest the author, random bits of knowledge or partly baked ideas ("What could have caused that civilization to disappear, Professor?" "Well, let me tell you about how civilizations evolve. . . . "). Remember that Theodore Sturgeon defined SF as "knowledge fiction." The ideas, even the sloppy ones, establish an environment wherein knowledge is important, wherein ideas can solve problems, wherein characters who think are efficacious.

In all types of popular fiction other than SF, characters act according to their feelings more than their rational abilities (only "cold" villains think "too much"). Even the tough detective and the gunfighter must have their emotions involved conventionally—only in SF is good smarter than evil. Good triumphs over evil in SF because the central character solves problems using thought and knowledge (usually technological). Even when the hero cuts a Gordian knot, he usually has to build or invent the sword first. And the triumph is all the more thrilling and satisfying if the solution is surprising and unusual—a crazy, far-out, wild idea that really works in context. This is one of the great differences between fantasy and SF— the fantasy hero triumphs through brute force or superior virtue, never through superior intelligence or knowledge (unless supplied by a tutelary spirit). In order to read and like SF, you have to be able to believe that ideas are interesting and quite possibly useful, no matter how strange and different they may seem at first. Just because an idea is not true at the moment does not mean that it may not be true under other circumstances, especially the circumstances that are the given in an SF story—and which might be real in another place or time.

A classic example of a science fiction story which arouses expectations that the rules are violable only to reinforce them is Tom Godwin's "The Cold Equations" (1954). This story enraged readers when it first appeared because its premise is that the problem is insoluble. It seems that a space pilot on a mission of mercy (delivering medicine to a plague-stricken space colony) discovers that a young girl has managed to stow away aboard the ship. Her weight alone will use up enough fuel so that he will not be able to complete the mission and there is no other ship available or near enough to rescue her. She must be jettisoned into space and die. The science and logic of the situation cannot be contravened except by a *deus ex machina*— her plight is milked for all its pathos; no regiment of cavalry arrives; she dies. The moral is that facts are facts, knowledge is knowledge, feelings don't change anything.

What do "The Cold Equations" and Kuttner's story about the drunk who invents a super can opener have in common? In each case a whole catalogue of ideas is presented and discarded, after examination, in search of a solution to the problem, and in the end logic triumphs. To get the effect of either story, you must follow the logic and consider the ideas as they occur. In this respect, SF is not different from the classic detective story in which the crime is solved through a proper assemblage of facts. There is in fact a whole class of "scientific detective" fiction that is in many cases indistinguishable from SF, except that it died out for the most part in the 1920s, at the same time SF was becoming self-conscious. These were the stories in which an arch-criminal genius invents a new weapon or criminal device which the detective must combat through scientific detection— this genre is still alive in the superhero comic books although in a degenerate form wherein the hero triumphs through moral virtue, since evil genius tends to make silly mistakes due to overconfidence. Minor exceptions aside, however, an unlimited spectrum of SF settings are possible in which wild and unusual ideas are the facts of daily life.

We noted earlier that an SF story about a new liquid rocket fuel would be uninteresting—while a story about a spaceship propelled by exploding a series of atomic bombs might be much better SF, since the idea is bigger and crazier (yet such a ship was in development, although never built, by U.S. scientists in the late 1950s and early 1960s—and they still maintain that it would work). To SF readers, the wilder and bigger and more unusual the ideas, the more gripping and intense is their involvement in the story and their interest in the ideas. Alien and future settings, technological devices capable of doing new things, humans pitted against strange and different problems in imagined situations—ideas generate the stories and fill the stories.

Within the SF field, you can escape from a mundane world into an environment where ideas are respected, discussed, the essential coin of the realm. It is not so much that any given idea is taken seriously by the field as that every idea is potential meat for discussion. Robert A. Heinlein, you will remember, made a full-scale attack on the preconceived ideas of Western civilization in *Stranger in a Strange Land*. In thirty years of editorials, John W. Campbell continually shook up the field by defending unconventional ideas such as slavery, Dianetics, psi powers, atomic power (especially before 1946), and a host of others. The field as a whole is an enormous repository of ideas of all sorts, but particularly strange, controversial, wild, and crazy ideas.

In the long run, perhaps the seminal influence of science fiction on our lives and on the lives of our descendants will have been that SF gives access to ideas that may become real and embodies them in a variety of scenarios for reality. Of more significance than prediction is the vision of alternate modes of life, of changed behavior patterns that the future might demand or permit. Heinlein's *Stranger* was a novel of extraordinary influence outside the SF community: Along with Frank Herbert's *Dune* it helped to shape the popular consciousness of the late 1960s as communal, sexually liberated, environmentally conscious. Powerful ideas concerning great changes in humanity are waiting in accessible form, clothed in science fiction. If you read them when you were twelve, you will remember them when you are older, even if you do not remember where they came from. You have a fairly definite idea of what the future holds in store right now, and you have gotten it from SF or from people who read or have read SF.

Think about it for a minute. For the first time in human history, most educated people know quite a bit about the future. It exists in three potentialities: most probable (worst)—things will continue downhill leading to disaster or depression or dictatorship; next probable (best)—humanity will improve through science and technology, raised consciousness, moral rearmament; improbable—an outside force (God, aliens from space, sudden mutation producing universal telepathy) will intervene and change the rules. Sane humans prepare against the worst and work for the best because they also know that both the best and the worst will happen. And everything we think we know about the future comes ultimately from SF, from Wells to the present. For all of us today, the future is as real as the past, and as different from the present.

The details of the future are going to be more eccentric than we can imagine. (Who could have imagined miniskirts, the Beatles, or Eldridge Cleaver's codpieces?) But SF writers have been writing about the energy crisis, for instance, since the mid-Fifties (Frank Herbert's first novel, *Under Pressure,* dealt with underwater oil-drilling stealing from another country's offshore reserves). Most of our large general problems have been dealt with for years and from a variety of points of view as SF, and the SF treatments have been read and filtered back into popular consciousness as attitudes toward our problems.

The earliest SF that had any significant impact was the body of nineteenth century utopian writings set in the future, bright visions of where social progress might lead. At the same time there were visions of technological progress, but until the 1890s it was the social visions that penetrated popular consciousness, right up to Edward Bellamy's *Looking Backward.* Then quite suddenly, H. G. Wells in England, Kurt Lasswitz in Germany, and a host of minor writers in the U.S. and elsewhere began to write of futures altered by scientific and technological innovation. And not all of these visions were optimistic. Whereas the utopian visions were undoubtedly influential, it was the anti-utopian visions of E. M. Forster, Aldous Huxley, Yevgeniy Zamyatin, Orwell, Jack London, M. P. Shiel, and, of course, H. G. Wells that really made us conscious of the future by basically making us scared of it in a new way.

Meanwhile, the new SF genre magazines were grinding out numerous stories about technology that would alter our daily lives and our world view. In the U.S., science fiction had absorbed and subsumed the whole utopian tradition by the early 1940s—it was where anyone had to go to find images of the future. Since that time, our future has been imaged and imaginable only through SF. Such is the power of SF that we can no longer imagine a future without scientific and technological change as a major factor. Too many clichés of science fiction, such as space travel and atomic bombs and atomic energy, have already become fact and altered our lives. We are now living, more or less, in the SF world of the future as envisioned in the early 1940s—and moving into the world of 1950s SF. In a way, the futurologists such as Alvin Toffler are more correct than even most of their group realize when they advise reading SF— somewhere in the literature are the ideas that will organize and limit our lives in the future. And those of us who read SF enough to know what the choices are will have, more than most others, the opportunity to make an informed choice among the alternatives.

Lest I overemphasize, however, the utilitarian aspect of ideas, let us back off and remember that only a minority of SF is about the near future (say, the next two hundred years). The majority is either about the third track future mentioned earlier, the improbable future, or about the distant results of the more probable futures (e.g., Walter M. Miller's classic novel, *A Canticle for Leibowitz,* which opens hundreds of years after a disastrous nuclear war). Only with distance can the SF writer achieve the scope to develop most big ideas (note that Varley's story takes place after alien superbeings have exiled the human race from Earth). Why write another variation on the near future when you have millions of years to play in?

The chronic readers don't really care so much for near future stuff. After all, they want entertainment, including the entertainment of big, wild speculation. And remember that most of the chronics are not the movers and shakers of our society. The chronics and omnivores are not really living in the present at all, are independent of or alienated from or rejected by peer groups. In a real sense the fans are enlightened masters who have no relation to mere present mundane existence—they play their godlike games and shun the world. Every once in a while they deign to notice something like the energy crisis—"Oh, yes, of course . . . that . . . "—but for the most part they can't be bothered with reality. They live on paper and ink in the realm of Platonic forms. You may be a concerned and aware citizen building a better life in the present, but don't expect much help from the fans. Even in conversation with one, it is difficult to elicit a response that is solid and to the point. You really have to read the literature. Afterward you may be able to conquer the universe—although you may not care to anymore.

Judith Merril, in a recent interview, states that she was very much aware, as a writer of SF, of ideas and their impact, and gives the clear impression that the writers of the late 1940s and 1950s were intensely concerned with the transmission of ideas through SF. "Back in the Fifties," says Merril, "I used to talk about science fiction as being a sort of encyclopedia, in the sense of the French encyclopedia, which paved the consciousness-ground for the French and American revolutions. And I felt that this was very much what we were doing, that we were putting into print and into words ideas whose time was about to come, making it possible for people to become conscious of it. Not laying out programs or ideologies, but finding the images and the metaphors and the crystallizations in phrases." She goes on to observe that later, in the Sixties, some of the ideas from SF became part of the public consciousness, often without awareness of the source. "I'll tell you, for me personally the ultimate and complete reward for any writing I did or editing or any time I put into science fiction was when I first met Tom Disch. And he said, 'I want to thank you, because when I was growing up in the Midwest, I picked up a copy of one of your anthologies; and growing up in the Fifties there, it was the first time I ever knew that things could be different.' "

Merril and her friends, including Katherine MacLean and Theodore Sturgeon, "felt that what we were producing was consciousness seeds, which were going to grow and expand." How? "I did really believe that it was a vitally important literature and was going to have a significant effect on society in my own time. I didn't expect it to have that by becoming big and popular, not even to the extent that it has become, by any means, but only by influencing people who would influence people. The basic concept that an idea that's alive is going to spread."

Certainly the famous astronomer Carl Sagan is a case in point. In a *New York Times* essay ("Growing Up with Science Fiction") he testifies that SF led him to a life of science after he became an omnivore at age eleven (he was ten when he first read Edgar Rice Burroughs's Martian books). He provides a catalogue of SF ideas in discussing the relation of SF to science, and concludes: "Such ideas, when encountered young, can influence adult behavior. Many scientists deeply involved in the exploration of the solar system (myself among them) were first turned in that direction by science fiction. And the fact that some of the science fiction was not of the highest quality is irrelevant. Ten-year-olds do not read the scientific literature." It is of immense significance to Sagan and to us that SF conveys "bits and pieces, hints and phrases, of knowledge unknown or inaccessible to the reader." These ideas can and have changed individual lives, and individuals can and have changed the world.

Not only scientists such as Sagan and writers such as Tom Disch but everyone since the 1940s has grown up in a world saturated with SF ideas. Margaret Mead, in her 1970 book, *Culture and Commitment,* suggests that people born during or after World War II grew up in a world so profoundly different from what came before that it is useful to think of them as native born, while everyone born before World War II is an immigrant here. In relation to prewar reality, we are all living in a science fiction world, and we instinctively reach for science fiction concepts to help us understand and to explain to ourselves what is going on. Science fiction is the natural context of our times. Robert A. Heinlein, in his Future History chart published in 1941, named the 1960s "the crazy years," to be followed by years of religious revivalism leading to a religious dictatorship in the U.S. I sure hope he was way off base. But Heinlein also wrote stories of nuclear power plant disasters and space exploration taking place in this time period—makes us feel a bit uncomfortable.

Where do we get these crazy ideas? From science fiction, of course.

III WRITERS, FANS, CRITICS

7 | Why "Science Fiction" Is the Wrong and Only Name for It

"SCIENCE" and "fiction" are actually an odd pair of words to be joined together in taxonomic matrimony. Science in our culture is very serious stuff— scientists are the keepers of the flame, the priests of the secret knowledge by which we live; science is truth. Fiction, on the other hand, is lies—lighthearted lies, entertainment, something to relax with when the day's hard work is done. To most people, "science fiction" sounds much too serious to be attractive as entertainment. And if it's *fiction*, it obviously isn't real science, which means it's probably nutty stuff about monsters from space and empires beneath the sea.

In fact, "science fiction" is not a pair of words to people within the field but a name, a concept, as specific and ambiguous as "Los Angeles." No two people agree on what Los Angeles does and does not include; the postal service has a different concept from the phone company; the state, county, and city governments can't agree; certainly the people who live there don't know whether L.A. means downtown plus Century City or everything from the mountains out to the beach, including the Valley. At the same time, it's no problem at all going to Los Angeles; one seldom arrives at the wrong city. Taxes get paid and the buses run (very infrequently). People in far cities curse the place and everyone knows where they mean. "Los Angeles" has no concrete definition that can be agreed on, but most people know what they mean when they use the term. So too with science fiction. And like Los Angeles, "science fiction" is almost universally misunderstood by people who don't live there.

In fact, science fiction, like Los Angeles, is a place most people already know they wouldn't like if they went there. Too much bad press. Science fiction shares with pornography the dubious distinction of being apart from art (the word "science" does it) and therefore lower than "real" literature. Simply put, if a work is literature it can't be science fiction (as if the two were mutually exclusive) and the label "science fiction" on a book or magazine denotes "not literature." There has been for all practical purposes unanimous agreement outside the science fiction field for decades that SF should be judged by its worst examples—and condemned.

Science fiction has been condemned as fascist, sexist, subversive, poorly written, ill-conceived, utopian, pessimistic, protechnology, antihumanist, and quite a variety of unpleasant names. There must be deep cultural and/or mass psychological reasons why so much energy was expended for so many years in efforts to make sure science fiction was never judged by its best examples.

One thing is sure: The science fiction world has expended a lot of energy in *support* of this condemnation. There is no real consensus in the field as to what the great works are or why— each chronic chooses his pantheon and argues it with others— and as long as the basic question of definition is unresolved, there won't be. This seems to have helped the science fiction world feed its sense of isolated superiority. Outsiders just can't understand. As in any clique, fraternal organization, or tribal unit, the initiated are in possession of secrets not lightly granted to others. Over the years, a fair amount of mumbo-jumbo has attached itself to science fiction and to the inhabitants of the science fiction world.

Advanced omnivores and chronics are in possession of a number of shibboleths, an entire code language both written and spoken, which can effectively exclude outsiders from conversation without proper initiation. SF authors are in possession of a huge body of useful clichés, in common use in the field, representing often rather complex scientific and technological concepts that have been explained in depth at one time in the past in one or more classic SF works and can now be simply alluded to in a contemporary story. Once, long ago, "spaceship" was such a term.

This mystification through language is such an integral part of the science fiction world that most authors and readers have forgotten it works that way. What it means, though, is that a mature adult confronting science fiction initially must either be able to call up (by association with SF films, TV, or other peripheral representations) enough of the conventions of science fiction to comprehend the basic language pattern or he will be lost, will have to expend omnivore-behavior efforts to "get into" science fiction. In this way, sadly, science fiction is just like medicine or any other special field or technical endeavor, unintelligible to the uninitiated because of linguistic mystification. And this feeds an entirely illusory feeling of intellectual superiority on the part of those initiated.

But SF is not, hardly ever, about science as theory or lab work; it's about technology, applied science, neat gadgets. The archetypal gadget of contemporary culture is the pinball or arcade machine. Who among us would not own one if he could? But they are pure gadgets and we cannot rationalize spending hard-earned cash that way, so we buy big cars, digital watches (Did your old watch actually wear out?), and other useful things. Note that toys, from Buck Rogers blasters to plastic Godzillas, taken directly from science fiction have been a major element in the toy market for decades, now perhaps *the* major portion. And technological progress through better gadgets has been a continuing obsession of American culture since Thomas A. Edison became a national hero in the late nineteenth century.

Science fiction is stuck with its name now, as it has been since 1929 (when editor Hugo Gernsback replaced the term "scientifiction" with "science fiction"), and though it seems unlikely to change, it will be illuminating to discuss the alternatives proposed and discarded over the years (and some of the names used by others before the field came into existence in 1926).

The history of the world of science fiction dates from the birth of conscious separateness, April 1926. In the nineteenth century, one occasionally runs across locutions like "the scientific romance" in both England and America, referring to authors such as Verne and, later, Wells. And we now know of literally hundreds of novels and stories published in each country during the century before the advent of *Amazing* that fit without any strain at all under the rubric science fiction, but this is a recent discovery, a brand-new field of literary historical research opened only in the last decade or so. Research has turned up such curious items as the following short article from the *New York Herald* of September 5, 1835, which is spooky in its parallel to Gernsback's announcement ninety-one years later—Has there really been a world of science fiction hidden from us for all this time?—and announced with a headline:

New Species of Literature

We learn that Mr. R. A. Locke, the ingenious author of the late "Moon Story" or "Astronomical Hoax," is putting on the stocks the frame of a new novel on a subject similar to that of his recent able invention in astronomy. . . . His style is nearly as original as his conception. It is ornamented and highly imaginative. He may be said to be the inventor of an entire new species of literature, which we may call the "scientific novel." . . . We have had . . . crowds of "fashionable novels"; but fictitious history, founded on the discoveries and scientific hypotheses of the day, has seldom been attempted until Mr. Locke did so. In fact, Mr. Locke has opened a new vein, as original, as curious, as beautiful, as any of the greatest geniuses who ever wrote. He looks forward into futurity, and adapts his characters to the light of science.

Gernsback reprinted *The Moon Hoax* by Richard Adams Locke in the September 1927 issue of *Amazing,* never knowing how uniquely appropriate the selection but knowing full well that Locke was "scientifiction."

Lots of actual discussion went on throughout the nineteenth and early twentieth century in prefaces and introductions and in reviews about this new kind of fiction, but when Hugo named it, the name stuck for the first time (although he didn't actually call it science fiction until June 1929, in the first issue of *Science Wonder Stories,* the second SF magazine, which Gernsback founded when he lost control of *Amazing*). The name competition included "scientific fiction," a term Gernsback had coined for the fiction in his earlier magazine, *Science and Invention,* "pseudo-scientific stories," "weird-scientific stories," and even "fantascience." Scientifiction remained in use until 1953, but from 1929 onward the name most of the fans accept has been science fiction.

However, the science fiction world has never been quite satisfied with the name, especially because the word "science" makes so many people uncomfortable and because the boundaries of the field are so ill-defined to begin with. At first, to be friendly, a lot of people in the SF world started calling it SF (*ess eff*) to avoid the breakdown into science fiction/science fantasy—after all, it's all one thing. But this didn't solve problems; it simply avoided confrontation—until the mid-Sixties.

It should now be clear that the matter of definition has only been a really hot issue whenever something or someone new and innovative enters the field. Invariably, the field has accepted whoever or whatever joins with it. However, a greater or lesser part of the insiders have always raised the question, "Well, yes, this new stuff may be SF, but is it any good?" The early answer has always been, after some discussion, "Well, it's okay, but not as good as the old stuff." The New Wave polemics of the Sixties aggravated the chronic readers of SF because Moorcock and Merril presented the new stuff as actually better than past SF. This was not traditional behavior, and certainly confused and upset lots of longtime SF people: They were pushed to the point of saying that the New Wave (discussed in chapter 9) was not SF at all (clearly an indefensible position), and/or that it was anti-SF and no good at all (defensible but not, in the end, leading to any greater understanding of SF or the contributions of J. G. Ballard and others).

Science fiction "means what we point to when we say it" is the famous thumb-rule of Damon Knight. Norman Spinrad, in his admirable anthology *Modern Science Fiction*, defines SF as "anything published as science fiction," i.e., labeled SF by the package. What these two "definitions" and others like them mean is that what science fiction means to insiders is the sum of all examples and all possible examples. Science fiction is every SF story written or to be written, the sum total of science fictional reality past, present, and future—otherwise indefinable.

The mystery of what science fiction is, is therefore preserved from outsiders. For, you see, one of the great unarticulated foundations of the SF field, perhaps the most basic at the deepest level of the field's collective unconscious, is that the wonderful, inchoate family of science fiction all know what SF is by intuition. Knight and Spinrad know, as the gorgeous subjectivity of their own definitions orbits around them, that to the field, further definition is unacceptable—disunifying, exclusive, potentially destructive of the fragile elitism that bonds chronic reader to chronic reader to editor to writer to illustrator to the most callow neofan.

Ah, but the desire to tame life through classification and subdivision (define and conquer) is no less strong among science fiction people than others, even though it may be a manifestation of the field's collective death wish, if our theory is correct. Ever since Hugo Gernsback pointed his finger at scientifiction in 1926, giving it a local habitation and a name, others have attempted to clarify the field by defining it or subdividing it.

On the surface, it seems a fine idea to an SF person to have a neat and comprehensive definition so that when outsiders ask what it is you are reading, you can tell them to go look it up in the dictionary instead of making inarticulate grunts and moans of delight and pointing to a pulp magazine or paperback, then realizing too late that you probably should have hidden the thing behind a copy of *Time* because this is going to be hard to explain. But even very early in the game, in the era of Gernsback, the defects of definition began to appear. Science fiction people—having no more common sense than the rest of us, from Sam Moskowitz through John J. Pierce—have continued to attempt definitions. And all of the definitions from within the field have been accepted only by the definers' close friends because every definition either excluded from the field one or more of the works that the whole field (or at least a significant portion of it) regarded as a classic, or at any rate as true SF, or on the other hand included so much fantasy fiction and other related forms that great hunks of Western literature were included that "everyone knows" is not SF.

Well, not to put too fine a point on it, most SF people are eccentric as hell in one way or another (see chapter 10), and it was necessary from the very beginnings of the phenomenon to be permissive about the oddities of fellow chronics, most especially the other guy's oddities of taste. If space erotica is really the focus of this chronic's habit, then you damn well don't define it out of the field and leave the poor pervert without a home and friends—or the next thing you know, someone will define out sword-swinging, four-armed Martians who protect their beautiful humanoid egg-bearing princess and ride across the sands of Mars having wonderful adventures, and because you know you love Burroughs with an unreasoning passion, you will be homeless too. So it is all science fiction because we all agree to say it is, whirling and turning in mysterious cycles and fashions, always incorporating and growing by inclusion, feeding on all science and all fiction. This innate heterogeneity is one of science fiction's chief literary and conceptual strengths.

And the mystic shibboleth "science fiction" has been the bonding glue of the field. The names of great fanzines of the past, *Fantasy Fiction Field, Science Fiction Review, Fantasy Times, Fantascience Digest, Amateur Science Stories, Scientifiction, Science Fantasy Advertiser,* and thousands (!) of others, devoted to science fiction/fantasy fiction/imaginative literature/speculative fiction/fantascience/scientifiction or any other appellation one or more fans hung on the field, all hold and have held the field together in a great maelstrom of energy since the very beginning. Science fiction, as Vonnegut says, is written and read by joiners. Not all of them are social enough to actually go to conventions or even (poor lonely souls) to talk to other people about the SF they read; but anyone who reads the stuff enough to know what kind of book she wants before going into a bookstore does in fact feel a sense of identity with the field, knows secretly and with a small chill of pleasure that she is in on something, is part of the extended science fiction family.

The final irony is that a definition useful for students and scholars was produced in rough form in the late 1960s and has been honed and applied by outsiders throughout the 1970s:

> A literary genre whose necessary and sufficient conditions are the presence and interaction of estrangement and cognition, and whose main formal device is an imaginative framework alternative to the author's empirical environment.

This definition was produced by Darko Suvin, the noted scholar, coined phrases and all, and it works all right for a number of critics, but no one in the field will accept or use it since it does exclude some treasured conceptions held by most of the field for decades (it doesn't mention "science") and besides, it is academic and therefore suspect, if not downright subversive, maybe even anti-American (Suvin is European and a Marxist critic). It smacks of the academy, of the mummification of literary energy—dry, dry, dry.

The very existence of a definition that was admitted to work fairly well would be a harbinger of doom for the field, for that lovely, permissive, eccentric, and friendly family feud that has been the science fiction surround for decades. So it is not really there as far as the field is concerned.

Of course the most divisive and dangerous harbinger of doom on the SF horizon is really money in large amounts. Science fiction has undergone stunning inflation in recent years—it is worth hundreds of thousands of dollars on the open market, and the field (no, worse, only some of the field) is about to experience the corrupting power of wealth. But that's another chapter.

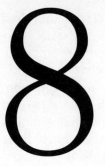

8 | Science Fiction Writers Can't Write for Sour Apples

Any bright high school sophomore can identify all the things that are *wrong* about Van Vogt. . . . But the challenge to criticism which pretends to do justice to science fiction is to say what is *right* about him: to identify his mythopoeic power, his ability to evoke primordial images, his gift for redeeming the marvelous in a world in which technology has preempted the province of magic and God is dead.

—Leslie A. Fiedler (from his essay "The Criticism of Science Fiction," in *Coordinates,* Southern Illinois University Press, 1983)

ALL THE wonderful ideas, the big hypotheses and powerful images, which so often are the main and abiding appeal in a science fiction story, have had a truly pernicious effect on characterization and style in SF over the decades. Nine times out of ten, the ideas and images have so fascinated the writers and readers that the rich and imaginative settings are inhabited by bloodless or flat stock characters familiar after a hundred years of adventure fiction.

So what? Well, the fashion in fiction that we admire since the middle of the nineteenth century has been that characterization is more and more the central task of the artist in prose fiction. By developing contrary to that fashion, for the most part in cheap commercial magazines and their market, science fiction has allied itself with the aesthetic of naturalistic, journalistic prose and fast-paced commercial storytelling, full of color and plot. The highest goal of the SF writers as a group, at least through the 1950s, was to achieve the slick (versus pulp) style of storytelling, popular from Kipling, Wells, and London up through Hammett, Fitzgerald, and Hemingway. And, of course, to sell their stories to magazines such as *Colliers, The Saturday Evening Post, Esquire,* and *Playboy,* for more than the penny or two per word prevalent in SF.

But the short story as a popular and commercial form died out in the U.S. in the 1950s, with the demise of most of the major markets for short fiction. Aside from the SF field, some detective fiction, and a very few organs such as *The New Yorker, Playboy, Redbook,* and, sigh, *Esquire,* short fiction survives today only as a noncommercial form in the literary magazines. And SF has survived not by changing so much as by staying mostly pop lit, in its own magazine and anthology ghetto. And of course in transplanted form in the media (where somehow the SF usually gets lost in translation).

One of the reasons that SF is so frequently transplanted off the written page into media presentations is that a mediocre SF story often tells in any form as effectively as it reads on the page. Since the standard for publication in the field from Gernsback (who didn't know English all that well but did know science and technology) through John W. Campbell, even to the present, has been clear prose that doesn't get in the way of the science fictional content, SF writers have not until the whole New Wave controversy in the 1960s had much encouragement to develop stylistically or to focus on fully rounded characterization. Many of the best of them did anyway, but sometimes in spite of editorial discouragement from portions of their market.

All this has been a disaster in terms of the image the field has presented to literate readers, mainstream authors, and most educated outsiders who have attempted to sample science fiction over the years, only to discover that most of the positive virtues which they have been led to equate with good writing and good literature are absent or wanting in many famous SF stories and novels. The one thing no one has ever accused SF of is overliterary pretension. A whole complex of controversies have eventuated within the field, among authors and readers, because of the "clear, unadorned prose" dictums of many of the major editors (and readers, of course).

What is almost never explained outside the field (or is passed off as nonsense by outsiders) is that SF has set for itself a progressive standard of good writing that has in turn established a variety of prose techniques eminently successful at communication from author to reader within the confines of the field, which is the primary aim of all written science fiction. The SF writer is first of all talking to his friendly and receptive audience. Communication to outsiders has always been considered secondary.

At worst, this has led to clever, plotted (but in every other manner underdeveloped) fictions. For example, even within the field New Wavers attacked *Analog,* perhaps their main paradigm of "the enemy," as a magazine mainly devoted to publishing engineering diagrams set in prose, not real fiction. And there have always been magazines and books recognized within the field as mostly crap.

The plain fact of the matter is that much of the best and greatest science fiction is not, according to most standards, well written. You can be convinced wholly that what SF does is good and valuable and interesting, yet if you cannot admire or like the manner in which it is done then you remain deprived of its finest pleasures. In this section, I hope to break the communication barrier between outside and inside.

If you are a writer of SF, you have to respect the facts of science. You have to know or take the trouble to learn the science particularly relevant to whatever story you write. However, by the early Fifties a writer could pretty easily fake knowledge of many areas of science and technology because the body of written SF since 1926 had developed a useful repository of cliché locutions. Phrases and words such as "space warp," "hyperspace," and "hyperdrive" can be used in any SF story to lend scientific verisimilitude (and that old SF flavor) without explanation or lengthy rationalization because other writers in the genre have already explained and rationalized them, often in great detail, in many other stories. The core chronic (and most omnivore) readership already knows what the terms refer to, how they work, and can fill in the rationalization from common reading experience.

Basically the writer can devote a higher concentration to what is new and different in a story and to exploring the implications of, for instance, a group of courageous humans taking a *spaceship* (one of the earliest of the cliché words) equipped with *hyperdrive* (which generally means a faster-than-light space drive) through *hyperspace* (that abnormal space through which a ship on hyperdrive travels) to a distant and alien planet. Well, heck, who knows, a writer might know nothing at all about how the characters really would travel, but the clichés get them from here to there and the usual concern (except in those special stories wherein the writer is introducing a new speculative device as the central focus) is those humans and that environment and their thoughts and feelings in it. And it is all scientifically possible, given the specific parameters of the story. If the writer knows that it simply won't happen that way or, worse, can't, then the writing is science fantasy—or just plain fantasy with a few technological details thrown in.

But it's damn difficult for a reader with insufficient background to use the conventions and cliché locutions in order to orient himself. Without reading experience, through which you learn the protocols of the genre, you can't tell whether you are reading good SF or bad, or fantasy that looks like SF.

Talented critics and readers have most often been led astray by their unfamiliarity with the reading protocols of SF. Their reviews and lectures often seem absurd, like someone discussing a play under the assumption that it conformed to the reading protocols of poetry. The writers and readers within the SF community who have done most of the reviewing and criticism of SF over the years have been most accurate and intelligent in their criticism and most stringently to the point.

On the other hand, the worst enemies of science fiction historically have been outside critics, often literati of stature whose taste is generally reliable in other genres, who have *defended* science fiction as wonderful, sloppy, energetic entertainment incapable of being good literature. The rallying cry to turn off good taste and wallow is insidious and powerful. Only one critic of substantial reputation, Robert Scholes (a leading critical theorist on the nature of narrative), has attempted to analyze science fiction prose styles to find out if and how they work—in his book *Structural Fabulation* (1975), he discovered that the prose styles function quite well, thank you, but no other critics have wanted to pay much attention to him on that point thus far.

So the level of reviewing and critical attention relating to SF outside the community is still pretty sad. You won't find any ready and reliable guides handy to what is new and good, nor much agreement on which older works hold up outside the field. The best commentary *in* the field, if you can locate it, is by Brian Aldiss (*Billion Year Spree,* 1973); James Blish (*The Issue at Hand,* 1964, and *More Issues at Hand,* 1970); Damon Knight (*In Search of Wonder,* 2nd ed., 1967); Samuel R. Delany (*The Jewel-Hinged Jaw,* 1976, *The American Shore,* 1977, and *Starboard Wine,* 1984); Algis Budrys; and Joanna Russ. These are all leading SF writers, and the bulk of their work lies in the back issues of SF magazines. (*Anatomy of Wonder,* 2nd ed., New York: Bowker, 1982, edited by Neil Barron, is the first full-scale attempt at assessment, and is only a partial success.)

Let us back up, though, and distance ourselves a bit further from the present state of criticism. I stated, in my discussion of wonder, that some of the *best* science fiction is not particularly well written according to any set of accepted literary standards, and further, that it doesn't matter much to the field one way or another as long as the story delivers. Recall C. S. Lewis's characterization of the sensitive reader of myths who hardly notices the words. Well, what I have maintained is true as far as it goes but now it is high time to pursue the matter further.

SF writers, editors, even the more serious-minded chronic readers right from the days of H. P. Lovecraft and Doc Smith, through John Campbell and his *Astounding* renaissance, James

Blish and Damon Knight, Algis Budrys and the Merril/Moor-cock New Wave, to the present have always stood for a progressive rise in the literary standards. And SF, in each decade since the 1920s, has indeed been better written as a whole. There has been real and substantial progress. But in every decade there have been writers of exceptional talent and ability, some of them at the forefront of the field and some of them almost totally unnoticed, producing work equal to or better than what is generally being published at present in the 1980s.

Just as in the macrocosm of English and American literature, where a Herman Melville or a Henry H. Roth can be lost for a generation, so in the separate microcosm of the SF field can a writer be ignored for years. And as fashions change, whole groups or periods of writing from the past are reassessed. When Campbell succeeded in creating his golden age in the 1940s, an almost knee-jerk downgrading of the pulp SF of the 1920s and 1930s occurred. His standards also excluded such major talents from *Astounding* as Ray Bradbury and Leigh Brackett, who published throughout the decade in minor magazines. Even Arthur C. Clarke's Stapledonian *Against the Fall of Night* and such writers as Kornbluth, Pohl, and Knight had to wait for the boom of the 1950s, with its new, broader standards, to gain major reputations. In the 1970s, most of the experimental writing of the 1960s remained out of fashion. Now, in the 1980s, there are signs of further reassessment, with the 1950s reigning as the "decade of classics."

Each past change in standards has tended to broaden the field and therefore improve science fiction as a whole, drawing in new writers and challenging the established names to higher exploits. But so far, no authors recognized for ability to evoke wonder have *lost* much ground, gone out of print, because the people who read them at age twelve are still in the field in sufficient numbers to keep their works alive—although time passes and substantial reputations are now dwindling. (A few, such as some primitives from the Gernsback era, have almost disappeared, but even they could suddenly bloom again, as L. Ron Hubbard did in 1982 with his best-seller *Battlefield Earth*.)

But the stunning fact is that writers no better than the

average in the 1930s can and still do enter the field each year, are published repeatedly, and are building growing reputations based solely on their ability to evoke wonder. And now is the time to say it outright—you must take the intentions of the writers and the demands of the audience fully into account before you call someone a bad writer. We have gone along thus far admitting that the level of prose style of all but the finest SF is not up to the level of prose acceptable in even the slick commercial magazines (those that are surviving today). Now is the time to complete our argument: Prose that fulfills the conscious artistic intentions of the writer (however unfashionable) and meets the demands of the market and the audience cannot simply be called *bad* and left at that. In many science fiction stories the prose style functions perfectly in place and must otherwise be ignored. This is the real point Vonnegut is making as he speaks in the voice of Eliot Rosewater, and the unarticulated point of all those critics who say they enjoy reading science fiction that is unpretentious and sloppy and does not aspire to "literature." As if the rubric "literature" were an award given by critics and reviewers, not by sensitive readers continuing to read it!

Let's look at two writers whose popularity has endured for several decades and whose styles have been abominated in or out of the field: A. E. Van Vogt and Cordwainer Smith. Both have in common an adherence to the colorful, event-filled, one-damn-thing-after-another technique of writing.

Cordwainer Smith's rhythmic, pseudopoetic ramblings wash over an allegorical (Christian) future universe ruled over by the Lords of the Instrumentality (the nobility). His self-conscious literary pose is undercut by a seeming lack of control over structure that is at once a Romantic posture and an oversentimentalized failing. Yet his stories are compelling to the SF audience for the evocative changes they ring on familiar and worn-down SF clichés. He is outrageous. More pointedly, at his most powerful he creates mysterious Poe-like images of half-realized but immensely suggestive transcendence.

Much more than Smith, Van Vogt is an insider's hero whose work endures, but presents a direct challenge to any sympathetic discussion of SF. The well-known critic Leslie Fiedler offers the problem in his essay "The Criticism of Science Fiction" (*Coordinates,* p. 11) without attempting a solution: "Van Vogt is a test case . . . since any apology for or analysis of science fiction which fails to come to terms with his appeal and major importance, defends or defines the genre by falsifying it."

Van Vogt is one of the easiest targets for attack ever to expose himself by publishing SF. And he is the author of a body of work of classic status within the field and is of enduring influence on later writers as disparate as Philip K. Dick, Keith Laumer, Charles Harness, and James Blish. His theory of composition, stated in "Complication in the Science Fiction Story" (as published in *Of Worlds Beyond,* L. A. Eshbach, ed., Chicago: Advent, 1964, pp. 53–56) is so eccentric that it bears quotation:

> Think of it [the story] in scenes of about 800 words. . . . If you find that you have solved your scene purpose at the end of 300 words, then something is wrong. The scene isn't properly developed. There are not enough ideas in it, not enough detail, not enough complication.
>
> Ever since I started writing in the science fiction field, it has been my habit to put every current thought into a story I happened to be working on. Frequently, an idea would seem to have no relevance, but by mulling it over a little, I would usually find an approach that would make it usable.

Nearly all of the million words of fiction written by Van Vogt in his first decade in SF are currently in print in the Eighties and so is most of his work from the Fifties, Sixties, and Seventies.

At the same time that Van Vogt was a recognized giant of Campbell's golden age, certain fans such as Damon Knight (whose essay, "Cosmic Jerrybuilder," was first published in 1945) were mounting attacks on his classics, such as *Slan* and *The World of-A,* on the grounds of bad plotting and poor style (and in fact bad politics—he is pretty much in favor of monarchies and elite social classes). Knight's essay, reprinted and expanded in the Fifties and again in the Sixties, gained in influence as Knight became the premier critic and reviewer of the Fifties and a leader in the battle for higher standards. No one has taken Van Vogt seriously as a writer for a long time now. Yet he has been read and *still is.*

What no one seems to have noticed is that Van Vogt, more than any other single SF writer, is the conduit through which the energy of Gernsbackian, primitive wonder stories has been transmitted through the Campbellian age, when earlier styles of SF were otherwise rejected, and on into the SF of the present. James E. Gunn comes closest to understanding the importance of Van Vogt when he says, "Van Vogt was creating the mythology of science, writing stories of science as magic or magic as science" (*Alternate Worlds,* New Jersey: Prentice-Hall, 1975, p. 163). The style hardly matters. And as Knight proved, Van Vogt's awkwardness is certainly easy to ridicule—but to do so without an appreciation of Van Vogt's virtues misses the point.

While literary criticism has never admitted complication as a virtue in fiction, complication has always been central to the mainstream of science fiction. This is derived from the focus on plot and story (above character, theme, structure, stylistic polish) and of course setting. The novels of Jules Verne were complicated by the insertion of immense amounts of scientific and technological detail. There is substantial evidence that Verne's Victorian audience saw detail as edifying and pleasurable. That dense and almost preliterate classic of modern SF, Hugo Gernsback's *Ralph 124C41+* (1911), has almost nothing to it but its complications. Lester del Rey described it in *Science Fiction: 1926–1976* (New York: Garland Publishers, 1979, p. 33):

> As fiction, it is simply dreadful. . . . The plot is mostly a series of events that help to move from one marvelous device to another.
> But never mind that. It is one of the most important stories ever written in the science fiction vein. It is a constant parade of scientific wonders—but they are logically constructed wonders, with a lot of keen thought behind them. The novel forecasts more things that really came true than a hundred other pieces of science fiction could hope to achieve. There is television (which was named by Hugo Gernsback), microfilm, tape recording, fluorescent lighting, radar—in fact most of the things that did eventually make up our future.

Obviously, Gernsback's book depends entirely on its extraliterary virtues. And Van Vogt most of all sums up and transmutes this part of the science fiction tradition and transmits it forward to a large and influential body of better stylists who come after him.

But the better stylists who come after Van Vogt are not necessarily better writers of science fiction. Note the assumptions within the SF field evident in the following quotation from *Of Worlds Beyond,* Eshbach's introduction to Van Vogt's essay summarized earlier: "The writer who wishes to inject complication into his science fiction will find much of value in A. E. Van Vogt's article. And after all, a story without *some* complication (if it can be called a story) is a drab affair indeed, with little chance of gaining a publisher's check." Keep in mind that this essay was commissioned for and included in *Of Worlds Beyond,* the first volume ever published on the writing of science fiction (significantly subtitled *The science of science fiction writing*). Also included were essays by E. E. Smith, Robert A. Heinlein, John W. Campbell, L. Sprague de Camp, Jack Williamson, and John Taine (a pseudonym for Eric Temple Bell, then one of the great living mathematicians). And notice that Van Vogt is no literary dilettante. On page 53 of *Of Worlds Beyond,* he states: "I write a story with a full and conscious knowledge of technique. Whenever my mind blurs, no matter how slightly, on a point of technique, there my story starts to sag, and I have to go back, consciously thinking it over, spot the weakness, and repair it according to the principles by which I work."

Charles Platt, in his introduction to *The Players of Null-A* (Boston: Gregg Press, 1977, p. xviii), surely the single best piece of writing on Van Vogt's work, instructs us on how to read him according to his virtues:

> The tangled web of shifting motives, suspicions, and loyalties grows ever more involved, against a canvas of galactic scope, until the whole picture becomes too large to be held in the reader's imagination all at one time. . . . The reader really must approach [Van Vogt] with a sense of acceptance and a willingness to stay caught in the shifting moment of action; then the flavor can be enjoyed almost viscerally, just as a dream can be savored so long as one's logical skepticism is held in temporary abeyance.
>
> To suggest that the [work] is best read in this way is not to denigrate it as a piece of fiction, since obviously it has the

additional serious content on philosophical and (perhaps unconscious) symbolic levels. Naturally, these aspects are best ap-
proached analytically, but to *enjoy* the novel, as an adventure, it
must be read as an adventure—entailing an attitude which is not
always favored by literary critics.

From this vantage, looking back on the science fiction of the
last three or four decades, Van Vogt and Cordwainer Smith and
a large number of others (notably Alfred Bester and Philip K.
Dick) have maintained the tradition of complication in SF.

The heroic efforts of Knight, James Blish, and Judith Merril
in the 1950s as spokespeople basically opposed to unliterary
style and in favor of the fashionable virtues of characterization
and thematic complexity, were wasted in attacking such as Van
Vogt. Where their efforts were effective and useful were in
praise of such fine writers as Theodore Sturgeon and in examination of Arthur C. Clarke, Ray Bradbury, Asimov, Heinlein,
and in support of such newcomers as Philip K. Dick, Charles
Harness, Kurt Vonnegut, William Golding, Gore Vidal (his
Messiah), Bester, Algis Budrys, Frederik Pohl, Jack Vance—all
those who were establishing higher stylistic standards for future
writing in the field. Ironically, in the 1960s, Blish and Knight
and Merril were all carried forward on the crest of the New
Wave, practically out of SF altogether—Merril, after declaring
science fiction dead and speculative fiction risen from its corpse,
emigrated to Canada and did leave the field. Blish emigrated to
England, where his SF had always been read as serious literature and proceeded late in the decade to write *Star Trek* script
adaptations and little else until his death in the early 1970s.
Knight stopped writing SF almost entirely until 1982 and began
editing his original anthology series, *Orbit,* which quickly
became notable for its stylistic sophistication and, on the heels
of that, for its lack of popular appeal to readers of SF. Knight
remains a figure in the field today, but when Judy Merril
attended a SF convention in Boston three years ago, her name
was unfamiliar to many of the fans. "Hah," I overheard her
exclaim. "I've been away long enough to escape." More than
any others, these three gave critical support to the classics of the

1950s. As critics, they increased the audience for new styles of science fiction in their time.

But if science fiction is to survive and grow in our time, it must not lose its Van Vogts and Cordwainer Smiths, who really keep SF separated from fashionable literature and open to new possibilities for complication. There must arise a new generation of critics within the field who will praise the new when it has virtue, while respecting the strengths of the old. The last decade was notable for its lack of any consistent criticism based on a broad appreciation for both the old and newer styles of SF: The critics existed (Joanna Russ, Algis Budrys, Samuel R. Delany, Sidney Coleman to name a few) but never developed the kind of thrust and influence over the decade that Knight and Merril and Blish did in the 1950s, or that the New Wave controversy generated in the 1960s. The most influential critic of the decade was Lester del Rey, whose dislike of any advance beyond the virtues of classic (1950s) SF was the bellwether of the 1970s. That he was married to the editor of the most commercially successful SF publishing program of the decade (Del Rey Books) only cemented the authority that he had already earned as a critic and "elder statesman."

What about the science fiction writers who can and do write extremely well, whose style bears comparison with the finest contemporary writing in the language? We have been examining those SF writers who are not stylists, attempting to show why they receive attention, praise (sometimes), and an enduring audience in the science fiction field. It is appropriate now to turn our attention to those fine writers who have suffered at the hands of critics in and out of the field for their "literary pretensions." The list is long and honorable, from Theodore Sturgeon and Alfred Bester through J. G. Ballard, Algis Budrys, Brian W. Aldiss, Michael Moorcock, Thomas M. Disch, Gene Wolfe, and a large number of others.

Until the early 1950s, the science fiction field was so small and the writers so seriously underpaid that the writing of SF had to be almost entirely a labor of love. The audience supported it with love and attention, but no significant cash. One would think, then, that this environment, so similar to the environment in which the contemporary poet or serious dramatist writes, would foster a species of Romantic artiness. On the contrary, the SF field fostered an attitude of commercial cynicism. Robert A. Heinlein is and was from the start vocal about his position as a paid entertainer, not an artist (or artiste). Science fiction was invariably written to sell—there was never any sympathy for the pretension to writing without achieving publication—if your work didn't sell and get printed, you were just a fan, not a writer. Fans write all the time and no one pays them for it. This situation was probably the healthiest thing that could have happened to science fiction, a crucial factor in preserving the vital field while other commercial genres were losing their audiences and writers; while poetry, for instance, became arcane, specialized, unintelligible to the uninitiated and without a general audience to support its publication. No SF writer ever left the question of audience out of consideration. After all, the audience would write you letters, send you their fanzines, walk up to you at conventions and tell you if you disappointed them. And praise you if you satisfied them. Few writers anywhere are so fortunate.

It is still true that most SF writers don't earn their primary income writing SF, but the cash rewards are so much higher today that the author's economic dependence on the core audience is lessening for the first time in the history of the field. Now, a successful SF writer may make so much money that he or she need no longer depend on a coterie audience or even magazine or book publishers for continued income (it has been years since Heinlein had any economic motive for writing another story). Starting in the late 1940s, an SF writer could make some significant supplementary income from SF—and many new markets were beginning to open. Bradbury and Heinlein began to have stories published in *The Saturday Evening Post* and *Colliers,* two high-paying slick-paper markets. Others wanted to follow. Van Vogt, Frederic Brown, and Jack Williamson had substantial hardcover editions of novels published by major publishers—and this became the dream of every novelist, soon to be realized by many. The young writers of the late 1940s, and the non-Campbell group from the magazines knew that they were writing better than their predecessors, knew that markets were expanding, that they could compete with the established big names and, perhaps, surpass them.

The center of this excitement and this consciousness of a higher level of performance was New York City and specifically a group which had existed since the mid–1930s that centered around the fan club called "the Futurians" (Donald A. Wollheim, Damon Knight, Isaac Asimov, Fred Pohl, Judith Merril, C. M. Kornbluth, James Blish, Robert A. Lowndes, Richard Wilson, and later a wider circle including A. J. Budrys, Harlan Ellison, Robert Sheckley, Mike Shaara). Those who were young writers then seemed often to fall under the literary influence of James Blish and Theodore Sturgeon, two immense talents and two of the finest self-conscious artists that the science fiction field has produced. (Also the influence of Lester del Rey, mentor to Budrys and Ellison, is often underrated.) There was a general awareness that something new and explosive was going on, that they were the writers of the future and that their work was already on a higher level than ever before in the science fiction field—a new dawning of prosperity, success, recognition was imminent. And it all worked out that way—sort of. They all made careers in SF, got paid enough to live, if not well, then well enough, and gained recognition within the field for their talents. But outside the science fiction field only one author, Ray Bradbury, ever got wide praise and recognition. Literary lights such as Clifton Fadiman, Christopher Isherwood, and other names now faded into history, praised Bradbury as part of literature, not science fiction. Note the distinction.

To give him credit, Bradbury himself never quite denied writing science fiction (as Kurt Vonnegut did successfully for years, to his enormous literary benefit). But he did allow his famous book, *The Martian Chronicles,* to appear in paperback (New York: Bantam edition) for nearly twenty years with an extremely complimentary introduction by Clifton Fadiman, which is devoted to denying that the book is really science fiction—sure, it uses the stuff of science fiction but it is actually the work of a literary man, not one of those SF writers; and Bradbury is quoted as saying: "Science Fiction is a wonderful hammer; I intend to use it when and if necessary, to bark a few shins or knock a few heads, in order to make people leave people alone." In other words, I don't think of myself as a science fiction writer so much as a writer who uses science fiction sometimes. And it's true. Bradbury is more a fantasist who happened to grow up in science fiction fan circles.

But any one of those younger writers of the early Fifties would have mortgaged their souls for that kind of literary recognition. What they had never counted on was that no matter how well they wrote, as long as it was labeled science fiction it was totally and completely beyond the literary pale. Not literature. What a numbing disappointment it was to the best writers in the SF field to find, by the end of the Fifties, that the only likely way to literary respectability was to deny the SF label. This is still true in the U.S.

It was never entirely true in England, where writing SF was and is merely one strike against you. The situation there is that a novelist is a novelist, but if you write SF you'd better be excellent or you will be considered a bad novelist, your work very nearly white noise. But remember that this prejudice is part of the essential background against which Merril and the English New Wave proclaimed the birth of "speculative fiction" in the 1960s, and started a literary tradition. If writers could just get rid of that damn frustrating label, then the big guys would finally take their good work seriously.

Lester del Rey presents an unsympathetic but on the whole accurate summary of this Sixties mind set, in his recent book on the history of SF (*World of Science Fiction: 1926–1976*, pp. 258–59). To summarize del Rey's observations, a number of SF writers in the 1960s began to think of themselves as artists, whereas the prevalent attitude for generations had been a legacy of the field's pulp magazine origins: that SF writers are crafts-men paid to entertain and that in the process of producing a body of work the creation of art is not excluded from possibility (after all, there was Dashiell Hammett and, in SF, Theodore Sturgeon, Alfred Bester, and perhaps others). The goal of these new 1960s writers was art and they agreed *among themselves* that they were in fact producing good art, that in fact their science fiction was really *the* significant literature of the day. Of course del Rey holds this attitude in contempt and against the traditions of science fiction as well as against the real case. But I feel otherwise: that the case is by no means decided.

After all, from the mid-Sixties to the present, high literary art in America has been characterized by one of its practitioners, John Barth, as "the literature of exhaustion"—all the stories have been told and retold, so that the only subject of fiction, the proper subject of fiction, is fiction itself—and we have seen a whole lot of novels about novelists writing novels, pretty narrow stuff, though brilliantly executed. It's hardly enough to keep the mind alive and makes SF seem very alive in comparison.

There is no doubt that a significant number of science fiction writers today consider themselves literary artists, and a large number consider themselves traditional paid entertainers. But because of the newer attitude, I believe the likelihood that a work of SF may be a substantial work of literature has been greatly increased. It is not my place to declare who the real artists are and are not. But looking back over the past decades, it is evident that certain works are outstanding in their execution and will repay a reader who does *not* have an initiation into the special pleasures that come from long acquaintance with the SF field:

Brian W. Aldiss   *The Long Afternoon of Earth* (*Hothouse*)
Isaac Asimov   *The Caves of Steel*
J. G. Ballard   *The Best of J. G. Ballard*
Gregory Benford   *Timescape*
Alfred Bester   *The Stars My Destination*
James Blish   *A Case of Conscience*
Algis Budrys   *Rogue Moon*
Arthur C. Clarke   *Childhood's End*
Samuel R. Delany   *Dhalgren*
Philip K. Dick   *The Man in the High Castle*
Thomas M. Disch   334 and *Camp Concentration*
Daniel Keyes   *Flowers for Algernon*
Ursula K. Le Guin   *The Left Hand of Darkness* and *The Dispossessed*
Walter M. Miller, Jr.   *A Canticle for Leibowitz*
Edgar Pangborn   *A Mirror for Observers* and *Davy*

Joanna Russ *The Female Man*
Robert Silverberg *Dying Inside*
Theodore Sturgeon *More Than Human*
Gene Wolfe *The Book of the New Sun* (4 volumes)
Roger Zelazny *The Dream Master* and *Four for Tomorrow*

This list is by no means exhaustive, nor do I think that, unless your reading tastes are particularly catholic, you would enjoy all these books. However, you would find strong literary talents, highly developed personal styles, character, thematic complexity—something to admire—in every work. Most of these works are held in high regard within the field, although several of the authors are more popular outside the field than within it (Delany, Ballard, Keyes).

By now you should recognize that there are extraliterary virtues in much of the best science fiction that give those works strong and enduring appeal within the field, although the works themselves may not communicate these pleasures effectively to outsiders, due to literary fashion both outside the science fiction field and within it. And you should be aware, although the fact has rarely been recognized outside the field, that there exist certain works of the very highest quality according to the standards of accepted literary taste. That these works have gone so long unrecognized is not a failure of the science fiction field but reflects an unwillingness on the part of outsiders to believe that searching for these works will repay the effort. Now you know more than they do.

9 | New Wave: The Great War of the 1960s

CONFLICT and argument are an enduring presence in the SF world, but literary politics has yielded to open warfare on the largest scale only once. And the woman who launched a thousand polemics was Judith Merril, author, reviewer, and anthologist. A charismatic personality in SF since the late 1940s, Merril was an active social figure in the SF world and a bearer of higher literary standards in her reviews. But it was in her anthologies that her crusading spirit was most evident.

Merril produced the annual *Year's Best SF* volumes from 1955 until 1965, the most important "books of record" in the field in those years. In them, she made it her personal crusade to break down the growing proliferation of artificial categories in the field (hard SF, science fantasy, fantastic fiction, and many others) by calling everything by the letters "SF." But this was only the beginning of her mission. In the late Fifties and early Sixties, Merril began to discover that this was only the beginning of her crusade. She began to discover and identify instances of good SF writing outside the

142 AGE OF WONDERS

field, not merely in an attempt to bring writers like Jorge Luis
Borges and George P. Elliott and Robert Nathan to the attention
of the science fiction world but quite intentionally to blur and
ultimately obliterate the distinctions between science fiction
and the rest of contemporary literature, to bring science fiction
back into the mainstream. In this she was opposed by the
prestigious John W. Campbell, who claimed that science fiction
is so comprehensive in its conception, possibilities, settings,
etc., that all the rest of literature is just a special case, and a
limited one at that, of science fiction.

Merril, no whit deterred, proposed in the early Sixties that the
field change its name to speculative fiction, redefining SF (*ess
eff*) to be equal to and congruent with spec fic (speculative
fiction, that term introduced by Heinlein in his 1941 Denven-
tion—Denver Worldcon—speech). She had a point in that no
one could deny that SF had never been defined. But as it turned
out, the field wasn't going to accept her as its "onlie definer."
What followed was the greatest battle in modern SF history, the
New Wave controversy.

To summarize six years of battle in a couple of paragraphs,
two groups of writers, almost all young and new to SF, took up
Merril's rallying cry and revolutionized science fiction by
infusing into the field the entire range of literary techniques
available to the contemporary writer of the avant-garde. One
group was loosely centered around Merril and the Milford,
Pennsylvania, annual SF writers conference in the U.S.; the
other (larger, more coherent and more radical) was centered
around the British magazine *New Worlds* (1964–1970), and its
editor, Michael Moorcock. *New Worlds* had reached the extreme
point, just before the end in 1970 or so, where it was hard to tell
the fiction from the paid advertising, it was so experimental.

For five or six years, New Wave and speculative fiction were
au courant in the science fiction world, but by the end of the
Sixties, Merril was a political refugee living in Canada, *New
World*'s British Arts Council grants had run out and the magazine folded, and young writers were beginning to admit in
public to being science fiction writers again. The science fiction
world settled back to digest and incorporate an enormous
transfusion of literary technique, the new blood of a whole

generation of diverse talents such as Michael Moorcock, Samuel R. Delany, Norman Spinrad, Roger Zelazny, Ursula K. Le Guin, Thomas M. Disch, Joanna Russ, and a host of others who would be *writers* by damn, not just science fiction writers. Poof! No more strict stylistic limitations on how a science fiction story is told.

What Moorcock and Ballard and Aldiss in England, and Merril and Delany and Russ and Disch and Ellison in the U.S., stood for—now that we have the advantage of a decade's perspective—was that SF is a special case of that category, literature, and as such may have as its goal the achievement of "high art" (the literary level of Joyce, Proust, Pound, Eliot). To the extent that, before the Sixties, SF did not aim for this level of achievement, we can perceive a failure of nerve in the field as a whole, traceable to the famous argument between Henry James and H. G. Wells. A good capsule discussion of how the James versus Wells bout influenced the development of SF is presented in the important and generally neglected essay introduction to the anthology *In Dreams Awake,* by Leslie Fiedler (New York: Dell, 1975, p. 16). The situation, complicated by a growing split between British and American SF according to which aesthetic dominated locally, is one of the unexamined roots of the present state of SF which future literary historians will have to untangle and examine. For present purposes only the surface situation applies to our considerations:

At the end of years of ever more serious disagreement between Wells and James, Wells finally was understood to stand for communicating ideas to a large audience through journalistic (unornamented) prose and James for a complex prose art that would stand for eternity like a cathedral, whole and entire, regardless of the size of the congregation.

Gernsback and, later, Campbell were prophets of the Wellsian aesthetic—as was Robert A. Heinlein. The first significant challenge to this was the Merril/Moorcock effort. And to make the matter more pleasingly ironic, we might note that it was not until later in Wells's career that he solidified into his aesthetic position, particularly in the Teens and Twenties. In the 1890s, as the radical, pessimistic young writer of *The Time Machine, The War of the Worlds,* and *The Island of Dr. Moreau* (enthusiastically praised by Henry James and Joseph Conrad, among others), and just after the turn of the century, as the author of utopian fictions based on technological progress, Wells was in no fashion the prophet of popular optimism he later became. It was as he moved further in the direction of optimism and popularity, as his position in society became more and more that of cultural guru, that Wells became James's enemy, evidently to James's dismay.

Robert A. Heinlein, of all the famous authors of SF between Wells and the present, most clearly and effectively caught the optimistic and technological problem-solving mode of the later Wells and adapted it in a body of work unparalleled in its popularity in the 1940s and 1950s. And Heinlein himself was a dominating personality in the SF field, perhaps second in influence only to John Campbell during those two great decades. But not only was Robert A. Heinlein changing in the 1960s (starting with *Stranger in a Strange Land,* which became a well-known underground classic), a new writer, J. G. Ballard, whose stories began appearing in England in the late 1950s, had become a focus of controversy.

The first work of Ballard's to appear in the U.S. was "Prima Belladonna," a sensitive, intense story of love and bizarre emotional states (more than vaguely reminiscent of Nathaniel Hawthorne's "Rappaccini's Daughter") set in Vermillion Sands, a surreal science fictional version of decadent future America. It was Ballard's first published work in Britain and was reprinted in Judith Merril's second annual *Year's Best* anthology (1957). Even in this first story, the kernel of what became Ballard's characteristic auctorial tone was present—a kind of tortured clinical detachment, raked into the surreal.

Most of the readership of science fiction (oh, well, why not admit it—most readers) are style deaf, can make only such gross distinctions as easy-to-read and hard-to-read, normal prose and complicated stuff, Hemingway and James Joyce, Wells and James, Robert Frost and T. S. Eliot or Pound. Science fiction, with a few notable but acceptable exceptions, remained until the early Sixties firmly entrenched in the Campbellian (in the footsteps of the later Wells) aesthetic of clean, precise, naturalistic writing for every situation. (The three stylistic mavericks of most high repute—Alfred Bester, Theodore Sturgeon, and Ray Bradbury—never repudiated the general standards and coexisted peacefully.)

Here is a piece of exemplary writing within a science fiction story, from the famous "Helen O'Loy" by Lester del Rey (a 1938 piece from Campbell's *Astounding*), quoted from *In Dreams Awake* (p. 147):

> She was beautiful, a dream spun in plastics and metals, something Keats might have seen dimly when he wrote his sonnet. If Helen of Troy had looked like that the Greeks must have been pikers when they launched only a thousand ships; at least, that's what I told Dave.
>
> "Helen of Troy, eh?" He looked at her tag. "At least it beats this thing—K2W88. Helen. . . . Mmmm . . . Helen of Alloy."
>
> "Not much swing to that, Dave. Too many unstressed syllables in the middle. How about Helen O'Loy?"

And a better than average example from "The Other Man" by Theodore Sturgeon, the man regarded as perhaps the best stylist of the day, which was included in Merril's 1957 *Year's Best SF* anthology (p. 236):

> He might have imagined her in old clothes, or in cheap clothes. Here she was in clothes which were both. He had allowed, in his thoughts of her, for change, but he had not thought her nose might have been broken, not that she might be so frighteningly thin. He had thought she would always walk like something wild . . . free, rather . . . but with stateliness, too, balanced and fine.

And here is a paragraph from Ballard's "Prima Belladonna," in the same anthology (p. 221):

> Harry groaned. "Don't you realize, this one is poetic, emergent, something straight out of the primal apocalyptic sea. She's probably divine."

It should come as no surprise that only a small minority of the SF field recognized Ballard as a revolutionary talent. To most of the field, he was an incursion of white noise. In the paragraphs above, del Rey's, Sturgeon's, and Ballard's characters are observing an attractive woman, but there the similarity ends. While both del Rey's and Sturgeon's prose is recognizably in the

Campbellian tradition, neither Ballard's prose nor his characters relate to this tradition. Ballard's characters live in a world where the inmost emotional states and the most complex intellectualizations are the surreal surfaces of their lives. They speak, act, and think abnormally. Ballard's stories are juxtaposed to reality in order to embody certain artistic insights which cannot be manifest within the confines of Campbellian SF.

Ballard continued to produce such stories into the early 1960s and then emerged as a novelist with four disaster novels, *The Wind from Nowhere, The Drowned World, The Burning World,* and *The Crystal World.* These and subsequent fictions made him the most controversial SF writer of the time. The novels were just as rich and strange as the stories; and, in an era when SF readers could still read every single work published, since there were still only about ten new SF books (at most) in any given month, and often less, the novels began to be talked about.

They were against the grain of SF, even called anti-SF by some, while hotly defended by others. In December of 1966, Algis J. Budrys launched a full-scale attack in the review column of *Galaxy* magazine against Ballard and his influence on SF, to which we will return. In 1968, Merril edited *England Swings SF,* a concentrated dose of the new British fiction widely reviewed in the U.S.; Michael Moorcock had already taken over the editorship of the magazine *New Worlds* in 1965. They raised the works of Ballard as the standard of the "new thing" in SF. Ballard was the avatar of change in SF and Merril and Moorcock were his prophets. Excitement gripped the SF world as open conflict raged and confusion reigned for years. It was the battle of the New Wave.

From the standpoint of the present, the whole great battle is best illuminated in the U.S. through the writings of the forces who summarized the opposition. (Everything went differently in England, where the controversy resulted in a serious aesthetic gap between British and American SF that persists to this day.) At the end, the opposition succeeded in turning attention away from style (and letting stylistic freedoms gained in the 1960s persist) toward an opposition between optimism and pessimism in SF.

In 1971, John J. Pierce published "Towards a Theory of Science Fiction," a rewrite of his 1968 paper, "Science Fiction and the Romantic Tradition." This was nothing less than an attempt to save SF by starting a "back to roots" movement. Pierce invoked Wells's film, *Things to Come*, which ends with a great optimistic rallying cry, as an antidote to the pessimistic likes of Dostoyevsky, Sartre, and Beckett in the contemporary world; he quotes at length from Robert A. Heinlein's essay on the science fiction novel in *The Science Fiction Novel: Comment & Criticism*. Ed. Basil Davenport (Chicago: Advent, 1959) which attacks "sick" contemporary fiction and proposes SF as a countervailing force; he marshals the forces of C. S. Lewis and Ayn Rand, Lester del Rey and Colin Wilson, James Branch Cabell and Donald A. Wollheim. Pierce's message was that true science fiction is in deadly danger. After nearly a decade of battle, true SF lies wounded and bleeding on the battlefield (page 31):

> The influence of the New Wave has led to a general collapse of criticial standards for science fiction. Mrs. Merril may have dropped out of sight, Ballard may be having trouble turning out any more of his "condensed novels" (verbal montages that have succeeded his catatonic disaster novels), *New Worlds* may barely manage to survive from one issue to the next . . . but the damage has been done. There is a mystique among critics and editors to the effect that science fiction cannot have any standards of its own, but must be used only as a "vehicle" or even as a "vocabulary" for some other art form.

There has been anti-SF before the advent of the New Wave, says Pierce, but never before has the critical establishment in science fiction embraced it. Even Damon Knight and James Blish, the paragons of criticism in SF, "eagerly curried favor" with the New Wave and Knight used his influence as president of the Science Fiction Writers of America to promote the movement. Pierce states (p. 30):

> "New Wave" [is] an effort to bring science fiction to the mainstream by sacrificing its values and traditions and substituting those of the mainstream.
> "New Wave" writers pretend to be breaking "conventions,"

but in fact they merely ape mainstream conventions. Ballard apes Dadaism, and surrealism. Disch imitates social realism, symbolism, Sartrean nausea and other clichés. Brian Aldiss, a convert to the "New Wave," imitated Robbe-Grillet in one novel [*Report on Probability A*] and Joyce in another [*Barefoot in the Head*]. New Worlds is full of pastiches of Kafka and Beckett. Ellison and some of his followers even incorporate the elements of supernatural horror. True, science fiction writers have borrowed styles before—but their plots and ideas were their own.

In "New Wave" fiction, science *always* leads only to disastrous results; humanity is *always* presented as evil, helpless and insignificant; the universe is *always* a nightmare beyond rational comprehension; and the philosophy is *always* nihilistic or deterministic. The "New Wave" writers claim to be individualistic, but this is merely a question of style and approach; the followers of Ballard take a cold and detached view towards their subject matter. . . .

Meanwhile, "New Wave" advocates deliberately misrepresent the history and traditions of science fiction: to read some of their arguments, one would believe nothing existed before 1964 but gadget stories and pulp adventure with cardboard characters, naïve utopianism and the like—that science fiction was devoid of serious ideas and problems. Science fiction has become a genre without honor in its own house.

Pierce quite clearly sees the New Wave movement as the great enemy of science fiction as he perceives it through the filter of his obvious limitations of taste and so on. His essay was the rallying cry of the old guard—hear again the poignant irony of Pierce's pained patience as he explains that they claim to be individualistic, those "New Wavicles," but their differences are not in the content or the plots, *where it matters*, but in style and approach. To Pierce and the whole SF field prior to the New Wave, style was synonymous with ornament, suspect, not often the subject of critical discussion and, when discussed, usually downgraded as some kind of pretentious excrescence. Of course, as we mentioned above, everyone knew that Sturgeon "had style," or Alfred Bester, or Cordwainer Smith, but how these stylists worked was not discussed. Blish and Knight, the best critics in the field, spent most of their time cutting to ribbons style that did not function in place, that did not advance the story without getting in the way. Damon Knight states his critical credo in *In Search of Wonder* (p. 1): "that science fiction is a field of literature worth taking seriously, and that ordinary critical standards can be meaningfully applied to it: e.g., originality, sincerity, style, construction, logic, coherence, sanity, garden-variety grammar." In his reviews, perhaps the most important body of reviewing in the 1950s, Knight stood for the transition from the "complex, cerebral, heavy-science-plus-action phase, toward a more balanced and easily digestible mixture of technology and human emotion" (p. 94). He observed and analyzed this change over the course of the decade, and produced works of his own which substantiated and legitimized in part the new 1950s SF, which is still the dominant paradigm of SF to this day.

The mixture of technology and human emotion Knight observed in such works as Sturgeon's *More Than Human,* Clarke's *Childhood's End,* the works of Philip K. Dick, Wilson Tucker, Pohl, Kornbluth, Blish, Budrys, Edgar Pangborn, Charles Harness, Asimov, Vonnegut, Sheckley, Vance, and Bester all represent what we see as the central image of science fiction at its best.

Pierce's fears were not, as it turned out, justified. What was dying out in the 1960s was not Pierce's true SF, which never flourished more than in the decade following Pierce's paper, but the Campbellian aesthetic, which was already dying out in the early 1950s with the advent of respectable alternatives to Campbell's magazine *Astounding*: *Galaxy, Magazine of Fantasy and Science Fiction, Fantastic,* and a host of short-lived brethren edited by everyone from Damon Knight to Lester del Rey. Every possible mixture of SF and fantasy was published in the 1950s. Writers went off in all directions and most of the names and novels and stories that publishers identify today as SF classics were first written and published. By 1956, when Judith Merril published her first annual *Year's Best* anthology, she continually referred to SF as science-fantasy to represent the broad and imprecise nature of the field as it had developed by the mid-Fifties. By this time as well, John W. Campbell was already saying that *Astounding* was the only magazine left really devoted to science fiction, that most of the rest of the field was publishing fantasy under the SF rubric.

Well, as we have seen, it was hard to tell the fantasy from the science fiction, impossible in fact, as long as the stylistic norm established by Campbell for both fields in *Astounding* and *Unknown* dominated. The reason that Moorcock and Merril could get a real argument going over Ballard in the early Sixties was that Ballard had finally and blatantly broken the stylistic conventions of SF and it was hard not to notice. And, of course, Ballard was more or less successfully ignored by the field for more than half a decade before the New Wave really got underway (his first stories and novels were praised generally from 1959 to 1963 or '64). And to give Pierce credit for some real perception, by the early 1970s he was looking back on more than five years of argument, and a substantial amount of amateur or failed literary experimentation, which had produced more heat than light but had certainly released a whole lot of energy.

As I have mentioned, Algis J. Budrys produced one of the classic diatribes against Ballard and the new mode of SF then emergent. Note the ringing scorn and righteous indignation with which his discussion vibrates:

> A story by J. G. Ballard, as you know, calls for people who don't think. One begins with characters who regard the physical universe as a mysterious and arbitrary place, and who would not dream of trying to understand its actual laws. Furthermore, in order to be the protagonist of a J. G. Ballard novel, or anything more than a very minor character therein, you must have cut yourself off from the entire body of scientific education. In this way, when the world disaster—be it wind or water—comes upon you, you are under absolutely no obligation to do anything but sit and worship it. Even more further, some force has acted to remove from the face of the world all people who might impose good sense or rational behavior on you, so that the disaster proceeds unchecked and unopposed except by the almost inevitable thumb-rule engineer type who for his comfort builds a huge pyramid to resist high winds, or trains a herd of alligators to help him out in dealing with deep water.

Budrys goes on to discuss this kind of science fiction in sarcastic phrases such as "the author's characters . . . produce the most amazing self-destructive reactions while making reasonably intelligent and somewhat intellectual mouth noises." And, referring to Thomas M. Disch's highly praised (especially by Judith Merril in a review in *Magazine of Fantasy and Science Fiction*) first novel, *The Genocides*, which Budrys believes is a Ballard imitation: "respectable friends of mine wedded to the school of science fiction which takes hope in science and in Man, [feel] that the book is unrelieved trash, ineptly written, pretentious, inconsistent and sophomoric. I personally feel that it reflects a deep and dedicated study of the trappings of a book [by Ballard] everybody says is good."

In conclusion, Budrys meditates that "it's not going to be easy to arrive at a snappy verdict on this general new kind of science fiction. For one thing, it's fundamentally different from most previous writing in the field—until you go back to H. G. Wells. . . . (In fact I can see a book called *Cartography of Chaos*, some ten years from now using the new mode as a demonstration that all U.S. science fiction between say 1930 and 1960 did not derive from classical sources, and that the importance of J. G. Ballard rests in his having singlehandedly returned the field to its main form.)"

For all his distaste and suspicion, Budrys does hit in passing upon the crucial fact that the early Wells was indeed pessimistic in tone, not at all the man who later wrote *Things to Come*. Wells had changed by the time SF was born, and the dark and pessimistic mode of Ballard and the New Wave was indeed closer to the classical sources of SF than the optimistic, problem-solving literature of John W. Campbell.

And now in the 1980s the New Wave is long ebbed, but the legacy of that controversy is that certain areas in which SF was shallow prior to the advent of Ballard are now regularly treated in depth. Budrys's friends, "wedded to the school of science fiction which takes hope in science and in Man," were actually wedded to clear naturalistic prose fictions in which the scientific knowledge of the protagonist was a priori adequate to solve whatever problem the plot posed (and said protagonist better not have too many disturbing personal problems to prevent him from fighting off the antagonist until the problem is solved).

Budrys's friends who maintained that Disch's *The Genocides* is "unrelieved trash, ineptly written" were wedded to a commercial magazine tradition that did not admit much stylistic variation and certainly did not permit practitioners any pessimistic assumptions. (As you will recall, there had been that absolute furor over the pessimistic little story by Tom Godwin, "The Cold Equations," in *Astounding* in 1954.)

Pierce and other survivors of the believers in science and in Man, were and still are unable (or unwilling) to appreciate the humane and literary virtues of any part of SF that might assume that science may be inadequate to solve a problem or individual humans inadequate to face the problem well. But, ironically, pessimism is still as unfashionable in SF today in the 1980s as it was in 1954 or 1966 or 1971. Most SF is still optimistic in its basic assumptions, but that optimism is not now as shallow as it often was before the advent of the New Wave.

The evolution of the New Wave in England differs significantly from what we have just followed in the U.S. and a rift still exists today in the field between the two environments. While Merril, Moorcock, and Ballard intersected at a crucial interstice in 1965, their lines were never parallel. Significantly, literary politics in the 1950s in England are the root of the divergent British line.

Important figures in the literary establishment in England began to accept and defend SF as valuable contemporary writing. Kingsley Amis, Angus Wilson, Anthony Burgess, Edmund Crispin, and others defended SF hotly, eloquently, and in public in the late Fifties and early Sixties, so that when the New Wave broke, the British were receptive to the new writers as part of a new generation. Still, of course, there were those who rejected SF as literature in England as in the U.S. So the British leaders of the New Wave invested their considerable polemical talents in denying that SF was in any way different from Literature. They felt a need to do this in order to achieve the final breakthrough into total literary respectability in their home territory. The U.S., of course, would follow, as it so often does, the dictates of English taste. Or so they seemed to think.

The assertion the British speculative fiction writers made that most disturbed and offended the chronics and omnivores of the Sixties and beyond in the U.S. was that "anything can happen in speculative fiction." That assertion, if accepted, would destroy the rule-of-thumb boundary between fantasy and science fiction, removing from active consideration by SF readers and writers that element of scientific plausibility and possibility of a science fictional idea "coming true." It was not just anti-Campbell (Campbell was still alive, editing his magazine, and very vocal); the assertion reduced the entire edifice of highly developed and rationalized locutions which had come to characterize and enhance the reading protocols of SF to a series of meaningless conveniences (at worst), or at any rate to convenient words and phrases useful in lending atmosphere to the work but essentially no more meaningful or significant in place than any other locutions. Thus were the classics of modern SF devalued in favor of the instant "classics" of the New Wave.

The British and American New Wave in common would have denied the genre status of SF entirely and ended the continual development of new specialized words and phrases common to the body of SF, without which SF would be indistinguishable from mundane fiction in its entirety (rather than only out on the borders of experimental SF, which is properly indistinguishable from any other experimental literature). The denial of special or genre status is ultimately the cause of the failure of the New Wave to achieve popularity, which, if it had become truly dominant, would have destroyed SF as a separate field. It is interesting to note the present state of British SF, where the New Wave did indeed dominate for a time. The present British writers of SF are either writing predominantly fantasy (Michael Moorcock) or a peculiar breed of science fiction which denies all the advantages of conventional SF in favor of intense psychological investigation of character in a rather sketchy or unrationalized SF setting, or of richly ornamented prose portrayals of surreal and/or grotesque settings inhabited by abnormal characters. Damn little wonder there.

At the 1979 World SF convention in Brighton, England, most of the younger British SF writers seemed a bit embarrassed in the presence of Arthur C. Clarke, who ignored the whole controversy and continued to write conventional SF throughout, remaining the most popular English SF writer in the world. This is in spite of the fact that he has never written a fully rounded character in his career, that being irrelevant to the strengths of his best fiction.

Eliot Rosewater (Vonnegut's great defender of SF in *God Bless You, Mr. Rosewater*) admitted that "science-fiction writers couldn't write for sour apples," but he declared that it didn't matter. "The hell with the talented sparrowfarts who write delicately of one small piece of one mere lifetime when the issues are galaxies, eons and trillions of souls yet to be born" (p. 27). The choice was clear to Rosewater: craftsmen or prophets, and he chose. But the issues are not as clear as Eliot had stated them and it is time we addressed some hard questions.

First of all, with a few notable exceptions, the best SF writers choose to write the way they do and all of the best of them develop quite individual and characteristic styles which sound their recognizable voices, strong and clear. Second, there is in fact as much range of stylistic variety within the confines of SF as there is in the mainstream of contemporary British and American prose fiction today. This variety was underplayed for decades, but the virtue of the New Wave controversy is that for nearly two decades now it has been emphasized. A large number of the best SF writers have produced works outside the field, often winning awards ranging from the Mystery Writers of America's Edgar to the National Book Award. But their major work has still been in the field and most often unrecognized outside.

There is no denying that most of the classics of SF from the Fifties and before are written in a fairly homogeneous journalistic prose. Until twenty years ago, ornamented styles were unacceptable to most SF editors (thus Ray Bradbury's inability to sell stories to Campbell). It was only with the breakdown of control by dominating editors beginning in the late 1950s that writers in general began to diverge substantially from the progressively cleaner and more precise naturalistic prose that was characteristic of all but a tiny minority of SF literature. This loosening of imposed control resulted in many prodigies and some grotesques: the New Wave, Heinlein's *Stranger in a*

Strange Land, Herbert's *Dune,* Dick's *The Man in the High Castle,* the advent of Roger Zelazny, Samuel R. Delany, Thomas M. Disch, Harlan Ellison, R. A. Lafferty, and a host of other individual talents. No longer did almost all SF sound somehow the same to the sensitive ear. The new writers of the Sixties most often took as their models the earlier mavericks Theodore Sturgeon and Alfred Bester, self-conscious stylists who had survived the earlier decades, and of course J. G. Ballard. The list is incomplete.

Frankly, though, in all but the best examples, the new variety of styles actually detracted from the focus on big ideas that had given power to the field up to the Sixties. The generation of the Sixties stood upon the shoulders of giants and for the most part copped their ideas—and wrote them up better than before. As the literary virtues of SF got more and more impressive over the decade of the Sixties, the ideas got spread thinner and thinner. This was, as noted earlier, the time when SF began to lose the excitement of space and space travel. The early 1970s are the years of what Brian Aldiss has called "life-style SF," novels and stories taking place in near-future SF settings in which the focus is not on the events of the story so much as on the life-style of the characters. Oh, yes, and there was a bust in the market for SF about this time (1969–71), in retrospect no surprise. There was very little excitement about the science in SF in those days and it looked to many people in the community (remember J. J. Pierce) as if the New Wave might have permanently damaged the field by deemphasizing science to the point where it became merely a literary device to enhance verisimilitude in future settings. Less wonder, to be sure.

Although SF has emerged from the 1970s stronger and more energetic than ever before, it seems that the raw energy of overarching ideas has been permanently tamed by higher levels of prose craftsmanship. There may never again be a fantastic and open repository of big ideas of the sort that space travel provided for decades to the SF field. Perhaps the bright hope for the field lies in the influx, in the last few years, of scientists and engineers writing SF part-time—perhaps they can provide, if only in rudimentary form, the "grammatical models" SF needs to keep growing images of power and wonder.

Meanwhile, the field seems to have reverted to the images of the mythic past, dragons and monsters and magic, even astrology, as the most popular source of inspiration. And the result is more fantasy and science fantasy than SF. It's beginning to get boring, too, pseudopoetic, pretentious, and basically foggy-minded. The fantasy audience seems to be a whole lot less critical and demanding than the inner SF community, satisfied with whatever magical images are given it and eager for more. SF has never drawn on and catered to an uncritical audience—the critical standards of SF omnivores and chronics have simply been different from establishment literary fashion. So the growth of fantasy and the fantasy audience may well represent a danger to the SF community as yet unrecognized and unarticulated. Perhaps the next genre war will be the Fantasy War.

10 | Fandom

EVEN AS the controversy raged over the New Wave and the extraliterary claims of the traditional writers were advanced, the outside critical establishment generally kept its customary distance. Every once in a while during those years, an eminence such as Kingsley Amis or Anthony Burgess would lend support and fuel to the revolutionaries, usually with a brick-bat or two at the old guard and SF in general. Fortunately, thanks to the loosely organized kingdom of science fiction fans, this ill-concealed disdain never diminished the ability of SF writers to develop their talents and be judged as their work progressed. Through fandom, a unique system for granting and withholding rewards had been created that continues to help science fiction flourish despite the literary world's unwillingness to become familiar with the goals and standards of SF

Fandom is the loosely organized realm of the science fiction fans. "Fan" has a special meaning when applied to the science fiction field, where it is not to be taken in the loose sense of aficionado, although that is an original synonym. A science fiction fan is not merely one who observes, who watches, no matter how worshipfully and attentively, as may be the case with a sports fan or a fan of popular music or a devotee of the works of Agatha Christie. SF fandom is made up of people engaging in one or more of the following activities: participating in local science fiction clubs or discussion groups; writing letters to magazines that publish SF; writing letters to other SF fans; attending regional or national SF conventions; collecting SF or related materials; publishing or participating in amateur publications about SF; publishing or participating in publications about SF fandom (not necessarily about science fiction directly).

A person who reads only SF, even if he or she reads a great deal of it, but does not engage in any of these activities is not part of the world of fandom and for the sake of clarity will be referred to as an SF reader rather than a fan. The great majority of SF readers—including most omnivores and chronics—in this strict sense are not fans.

Fans make up only a small part, perhaps 5 percent, of the SF audience. However, they play a central and crucial role in making the SF field what it is. Without fandom, SF might never have established itself as a genre, might well have perished long ago. The activities of fans have kept it alive and vigorous.

Local clubs and discussion groups were promoted by Hugo Gernsback in the late 1920s to focus support of *Amazing Stories.* They have repeatedly flourished and disappeared throughout the history of the field across the whole English-speaking world, gathering local SF readers together into groups and providing foci for SF-related activities. Even today, many local groups exist, some large and decades-old, some young and transitory— it only takes one fan to start such a group, to gather like-minded locals into a group where one makes "science fiction friends."

The nuclei of the earliest SF clubs were those readers who wrote letters of commentary to the SF magazines and thus announced their existence and interest. Over the years, letters to the magazines have become and remained one of the centers of fan activity, the traditional form of audience response and communication to magazine SF. And these letters, often published in the extensive letter columns of the magazines themselves, rapidly led to personal correspondence among the letter writers, direct communication between fans.

Fans are often indefatigable letter writers and maintain a number of active exchanges of letters with other fans around the world, many of whom they see in person only once or twice a decade, some of whom they never have met in the flesh. Yet a fan's correspondents may be among her or his closest and most intimate friends, science fiction friends because they made contact through science fiction, even though SF may literally never be discussed in the letters. Since the 1930s, fans have traveled all over the country, and the world on many occasions, with the sole purpose of seeing some of their SF friends in person. Part of the impetus for early SF conventions came from the opportunity such gatherings provided to meet unseen friends—and enemies too, for the fan community has always been a hotbed of disagreement among factions representing differing attitudes toward SF and toward fandom.

The stories of the early SF conventions that have come down to the present through such fan histories as Sam Moskowitz's *The Immortal Storm* (please note the implications of such a title) and Harry Warner, Jr.'s, two volumes, *All Our Yesterdays* and *A Wealth of Fable,* are filled with crazy stunts, love affairs, political squabbles, conflict, desperate seriousness, acts of heroism and generosity, all the drama of confronting in the flesh people whose lives are intimately entwined with yours, but whom you rarely see. No other phenomenon of the SF field points toward its unique nature so directly as does the SF convention, where from the beginning fans and professionals mixed and confronted each other and themselves. Conventions today are the most visible SF activity. As was discussed in chapter 1, conventions have now grown in number and size to the point where attendance is often in the thousands and there are multiple conventions available to attend in different parts of the U.S. on nearly every weekend of the year; thus convention attendance has become one of the most frequent fan activities, and perhaps the primary conduit of SF readers into fandom nowadays. Convention activities (the personal interactions as well as the program) are a constant subject of discussion in correspondence among fans and in the amateur magazines.

While the collecting of SF magazines, books, artwork, and other paraphernalia may be pursued in isolation, it has most often led to communication with fans and other fan activities. In the early days of the field, each issue of every magazine was a rare occurrence, to be treasured and preserved, read by you and your friends. Books containing or devoted to SF were published infrequently, quickly becoming scarce and desirable. As the field has grown, specialty book publishers were founded, such as Arkham House, Fantasy Press, and Gnome Press, to publish in permanent form the important authors of the field for the fans who preserved and collected the material. Now there are and have been for years a variety of book dealers, both mail order and those operating specialized open stores, who serve as sources for SF material to read and collect, and as conduits for information about the activities of fans and collectors. Again, one may be a reader and collector without being a fan, but collecting is a characteristic fan activity. The degree of a collector's involvement with other fans determines whether or not that collector is a fan. A fan is someone knowingly involved in "fandom," the world of fans.

The publication of amateur magazines devoted to science fiction began in the early 1930s as a means of communication and self-expression among fans beyond letter writing. Newsletters, public letters, magazines of fiction and nonfiction were spawned in significant numbers and formed an enduring bond among fans who participated in these publications. The market for SF was small and the fan magazines became proving grounds for neophytes and homes for the professionals whose material could not find a niche in the few paying markets. The most ambitious of these magazines did and still do publish a fair percentage of writing of professional quality. A fan might establish his identity in the field by producing writing or art for one of these magazines, or indeed by publishing such a magazine; might indeed become well known nationally or internationally among fans and professionals even today.

On the other hand, a number of magazines that developed at the same time and established a parallel tradition, evolved from the habit of personal correspondence (the "fannish" fanzines). This second variety of amateur magazine focuses entirely on the activities of the fans themselves, their daily lives and interactions. Science fiction may be mentioned or not. For the segment of fandom whose primary connection with the SF field is through these amateur magazines, the activity of fandom is an end in itself. Some profess that they no longer read SF at all, although the written matter of the field provided for their original entry into fandom.

Fandom has a history and traditions, a legacy of in-jokes and a specialized vocabulary, politics, mores: a culture. The evolution of fandom from small groups and isolated individuals in the early 1930s to the huge amorphous numbers of the 1980s is marked by enduring names such as Forrest J. Ackerman, Donald A. Wollheim, Sam Moskowitz, Frederik Pohl, Wilson (Bob) Tucker, David Kyle, Julius Schwartz, and others, whose titanic teenage personalities, their idealism, feuds, and jokes dominated the earliest fan eras—now generally referred to as First Fandom. They waged wars through correspondence, in fanzines and in person, sometimes lived together in what we would now call communes, promulgated philosophies and ideas, disrupted each other's attempts at organization. They played jokes on one another, the kind that can flourish only when a group is widely dispersed and communicates almost entirely by mail, the kind that teenage boys play (until the 1940s, there just weren't any women in fandom to speak of). The fans of the 1930s established traditions that have endured to this day. They set the tone.

The activities of the early fans came to define the true fan as opposed to the reader of SF. Their aspirations to the rank of professional and their success at attaining pro status made fandom the "farm team" system of the SF field. Many of the second and later generations of SF writers, for instance Ray Bradbury, Isaac Asimov, Frederik Pohl, Damon Knight, and James Blish, came out of fandom. They learned its lingo, its attitudes, traditions, and aspirations.

The language employed by fans is a written language full of typographical tricks, contractions, acronyms, and initialese, a shorthand including coinages and borrowings from SF used as shibboleths to identify a text as a fan text and used from common communication among fans. Here are some examples

loosely based on a classic fannish reference volume by Jack
Speer called, of course,

FANCYCLOPEDIA (1945)

ANGLOFAN—a fan living in the U.K.

APA—Amateur Press Association. A group of people who
publish fanzines and send them to an official editor
who assembles them and mails a copy of each to
each member in a regular bundle. Members comment on each other's fanzines in a kind of group
discussion.

BACOVER—the back cover of a magazine.

BHEER—beer, as in "Bheer is the only true Ghod."

BEM—Bug-Eyed Monster. The first bit of fan slang to get
into *Funk & Wagnalls Dictionary*.

BLOG—the (nonexistent) preferred drink of fans. Fan
parties and conventions often feature noxious con-
coctions invented for the occasion under this rubric.

CON—a gathering of fans from various localities. When
the numbers are larger than a handful, short for
convention.

CORFLU—correction fluid, used to correct errors on mimeograph stencils. Fan magazines are traditionally
produced on a mimeograph.

DNQ—Do Not Quote. Indicates a secret, something not to
be repeated.

EGOBOO—that which boosts the ego. The reward of fan
activity, usually seeing your name in print, especially but not necessarily in a favorable context.

ET—an extraterrestrial being. (Now, of course, no longer
limited to fandom since the movie.)

EYETRACKS—when you read a new book you get eyetracks
all over it and it is no longer in mint condition.

FAKE-FAN—one who hangs around with fans and enjoys
their company but takes no active part in fandom
and may not even be a reader of SF.

FANAC—the traditional activities of fans.

FANNISH—of or pertaining to fans. Used to distinguish a

form of activity from the professional or from aspiration to the professional, or even relation to the professional. A fannish fanzine is a publication about SF fandom (not necessarily about SF at all).

FANZINE—a fan publication, an amateur magazine published by fans.

FIAWOL—Fandom Is A Way Of Life.

FIJAGH—Fandom Is Just A Goddamn Hobby.

FILLER—words stuck in to fill up empty space, especially leftover space on a fanzine page, traditionally bits written by the editor, pieces of wit or wisdom or silliness. One of the art forms of fandom.

FMZ—fanzines.

GAFIA—Get Away From It All. Verb—gafiate. Said of an active fan who abandons all fannish activities out of distraction or loss of interest, and ends his/her contact with the fannish world. It is possible to return to fandom after an extended period of gafiation; but of course many gafiates are never heard from again.

GREEPS, CROTTLED—a legendary foodstuff, first introduced in a 1953 filler: "But if you don't like crottled greeps, what did you order them for?"

ILLO—illustration.

MACROCOSM—the mundane, nonfannish world, as opposed to fandom, the *Microcosm*.

MUNDANE—a person who is not a fan.

NEO—a person new to fandom. For the first year or so in fandom, a person is expected to exhibit neofan (brash and noisy) characteristics.

ONE-SHOT—a fanzine produced (perhaps written as well) at a single session. Strictly speaking, such a fanzine is intended to have only one issue.

SERCON—serious constructive. Refers to an attitudinal disposition to improve fandom and/or SF. The term has come to be the antonym of fannish—the academic criticism of SF in recent years is "too sercon."

SIMPLIFIED SPELLING (SIMPLIFYD SPELNG)—the practice of

eliminating silent letters, e.g., though/tho, through/thru, or substituting phonetically to condense. This form of shorthand probably entered fandom from the pre-(fan)historic SF novel by Hugo Gernsback, *Ralph 124C41+* ("one to foresee for one, plus"—the "plus" was a silent honorific). Forrest J. Ackerman, a leading popularizer of this mode in fan writing, is "4e" or "4sj."

TWONK'S DISEASE—the ultimate affliction: fallen armpits.

Fan vocabulary is filled with such words and practices, through which individual fans create their own fan personae and by which they communicate with others. It is not really difficult to pick up most of the lingo quickly and to begin to develop a science fiction persona, a fan personality of your very own.

In chapter 1, I expended some effort describing aspects of SF conventions and analyzing the experience of an attending reader or fan. Now that we are looking more closely at fandom, I should note that there are many levels of involvement in the contemporary event. With the enormous growth in convention attendance in the 1970s, it became an attractive social thing in some cases for a nonreader (sometimes politely called a "fringe fan" rather than a "mundane") to attend conventions to drink, smoke dope, and have sex, and pretty much ignore everything else. But the most confusing problem has been the huge influx of neofans into the convention environment without enough more experienced fans to help them to become acculturated. Thus the traditional fannish atmosphere has often been diluted and thinned, if not polluted. The changes are discussed and debated throughout fandom today. And with the recent near-bankruptcy of the 1983 Worldcon, the crisis point has arrived. There will be changes soon. The larger conventions have actually resulted in discouraging fans from pursuing the traditional task of further developing one's science fiction persona by social interaction with other fans, especially with the older and more experienced ones.

For goodness sake, it takes all the time of between twenty and a hundred volunteer fans just to run one of the larger conventions, and hundreds to run the huge annual World Convention. They interact with each other but not with the attendees very much. So as conventions have grown and become a mass and leveled activity, other aspects of fandom have become all the more important for the young fan attempting to establish a fannish identity. The most important of these is participation in (publishing, reading, writing for or to) the fanzines.

In the first two decades of fandom, more than ten thousand fanzines rolled from the fan presses, from single issue postcards to well-printed little magazines. It has been estimated that there were never more than 500 fans in fandom in the 1930s, 1,000 in the 1940s, perhaps 5,000 in the world (2,000 in the U.S.) by 1959. No generally available bibliographic work beyond 1950 has been published because the number of fanzines has increased virtually beyond tabulation. It is rumored that Bruce Pelz, a prominent fan, is keeping track, though.

Simply attempting to describe fanzines as a class is difficult, given the numbers and diversity. Certain general observations do apply: Most often, a fanzine is a mimeographed amateur magazine (yes, some are offset, but mimeo is traditional) typed onto stencils by the editor and publisher, with help from fan friends, written by the editor and friends, with regular features such as an editorial essay, one or more other essays, one or more pieces of amateur fiction, illustrations and cartoons, reviews of books, magazines, other SF materials, and a letter column in which the best letters received since the last issue are printed. Not infrequently, the letter column absorbs a major portion of the issue.

The entire contents of a fanzine may be devoted to a narrow focus such as *Star Trek* or the Darkover stories of Marion Zimmer Bradley, or to a broader but still restricted area such as SF by or concerning feminists, sword-and-sorcery fiction, film SF or SF comics. A fanzine may be devoted to a general mix, often including science fiction-related topics, fannish topics (such as a convention report), and topics not directly related to either (music, movies, politics, nostalgia, personal travels, etc.).

No fanzine that did not aspire to professional status has ever had a circulation much over a thousand copies, and most of the early famous fanzines have had circulations of 100 to 600, and are now treasured items in fannish collections. With very few exceptions, all the great fanzines of the past have been general interest mixtures, given unique ambiance by the strong personality of the editor(s). A successful fan editor creates a new Gestalt personality through effective assemblage of the parts of his or her fanzine. The most influential people in fandom at any given moment are its better fan editors.

On the other hand, the superstars of fandom are the humorists, the great fan writers such as Robert Bloch, Bob Tucker, Bob Shaw, Walt Willis, and others whose work has appeared in hundreds of fanzines over the decades (I include, of course, the fan cartoonists such as William Rotsler, Arthur Thompson (ATom), Tim Kirk, Bjo Trimble, Steve Stiles, Lee Hoffman, Stu Schiffman, Alexis Gilliland, and others). A fan editor's success at attracting material from the great humorists is a sure mark of approach to the Parnassus of fandom. As is, of course, attracting material from the big name professional SF writers of the era (specifically including letters of comment on issues—these announce that you are good enough and important enough to attract their attention).

In recent years, a number of leading fanzines have escalated out of fandom into the ranks of professional or semipro magazines, whose subscription lists and ads may contribute significantly to the support of the editor/publisher. They have circulations in the low thousands and are often sold in bookstores. Titles such as *Locus, Starship, Thrust, Shayol, SF Review, Fantasy Newsletter, Whispers* are printed, not mimeographed, contain a high proportion of material written by professionals, and are all valuable contributions to the SF field, read alike by readers of SF and fans. But they are not in the traditional sense fanzines, although they often appear on the ballot for best fanzine awards—a source of concern to fans throughout the last decade and which has led to the establishment of a new category of "semiprofessional" in the Hugo Awards in 1984. It is obvious upon comparison that the editorial tone and rejection of fannish vocabulary in these magazines denotes an intention to reach an audience of SF readers and professionals, a larger audience of course than fandom. These publications are still the most influential medium today for the transmission of fan opinions and attitudes to the wide audience of SF readers and should not be ignored by someone attempting to understand the SF field. It is just that the personae projected through these magazines are leveled and generalized.

What motivates the fan, the point of fan activity, is the construction, finishing, and exhibiting of a fan persona through collecting, convention appearances, and writings and other active contributions to the publishing of fanzines. What makes the development of this persona possible is the fact that fandom is a microcosm, a private, limited world with its own rules and mores, small enough so that some sense of belonging is within the reach of every fan who wants to be a part of it.

The population of fandom at a given moment reflects quite well the demographics of the population of the larger SF audience. Because the pressures of daily life (especially the economic demands) are less on people under the age of twenty-one, the majority of fans are teenagers and young adults. Yet since a mature and experienced body of older fans and a corpus of past fanzines exist, the traditions of fandom remain strong.

Among the large number of professionals who have become professionals after spending time in fandom, a great many have maintained active status in fandom throughout their careers by simply continuing their fannish activity, along with their professional careers. A few, such as Wilson Tucker and Robert Bloch, are perhaps more famous in the SF field as fans than as authors, in spite of long and distinguished professional careers. This intimate connection between fan and professional, as we have noted earlier, is one of the significant factors generally unknown to outsiders and so has ordinarily made the SF field difficult or impossible to understand. Fandom is a kind of invisible empire, unless you know how to look at it. Again, I am reminded of Thomas Pynchon's "undergrounds" in *The Crying of Lot 49* mentioned in chapter 1.

Perhaps the best way for an outsider to approach an understanding of the interaction of fans and professionals in the SF field is to overstate the case and say that the fans are the peers of the writers and editors, and exert steady peer-group pressure on them to conform to the standards and traditions of SF and to raise those standards in particular ways. Even the professional writers who come from the ranks of SF readers, not fandom, are rapidly made aware of fandom and take it into account when thinking about the audience for their works. There are cases of professionals, such as Barry N. Malzberg, who deny any influence from fandom and deplore its standards. Yet even they are conscious of fandom and sensitive to it. Writers who are totally unaware of fandom and publish SF, while they may reach a fair audience, in turn tend to be ignored or ridiculed by fans and have a harder time finding any substantial popularity among the other readers of SF. A writer who has never been a regular science fiction reader is an almost certain failure in the field, though not necessarily to outside critics and readers, for what by now must be obvious reasons.

A present or former fan or not, the SF writer is aware of a palpable and immediate audience. She meets them at conventions, they write her letters, send her fanzines that mention her and her work, respond in a fashion and in significant numbers unknown in any other field of literature. The fans are the SF writer's friends as well as the core of the SF audience, whose approval indicates wider support among the general readers of SF, whose disapproval is to be risked only with care and, perhaps, at great cost.

Just as a fan is expected to respond to SF, so the writer is expected to respond to the existence of fandom. An SF writer, to gain the support of the fans, is expected to appear at conventions (although not necessarily on the formal program) and interact personally with the fans; he is expected to answer personal correspondence from fans and to participate in some manner in fan publications. As stated above, a pro can confer recognition and fannish ego gratification upon a fan merely by writing a postcard or letter of comment to a fanzine. A professional who creates a benign persona with regard to fandom is assured of widespread and long-term support from the fan community.

Given the foregoing, it is easy to understand that one aspect of the antipathy in fandom to the growing attention that literary critics and academics have been paying to SF in the last decade or so is that such attention from outside the field must interfere with fandom's demand upon the writers for primary consideration. This is the first substantial challenge to the primacy and authority of fandom in the history of the field. And while this attitude has never to our knowledge been articulated in fandom, the situation has been grave for a number of years now.

Let us pass on, for the moment, to an examination of the negative aspects of fandom. The feuds and conflicts mentioned earlier and described in pompous and grandiloquent fashion in Moskowitz's *The Immortal Storm* are analyzed in Damon Knight's review of the work as "European power politics in a hatbox—scaled down, but still a politics of force, deceit and treachery. The same types emerged: the Booster, the Organizer, who frequently became the Wrecker." (Damon Knight, *In Search of Wonder,* op. cit., p. 162.) Fan politics are often bitter and divisive. In 1939, on the occasion of the first World SF convention in New York, six leaders of the Futurians, a prominent fan club, were refused admittance (including Donald A. Wollheim, C. M. Kornbluth, and Frederik Pohl) in a political act that is remembered with rancor to this day. Fan politics is a serious game and the losers sometimes pay inordinately.

To an outsider who sees fandom as nothing more than a time-consuming hobby, there is no more sense in it than collecting back issues of the *National Geographic* or, worse, nostalgia items. Fan activity is indeed time-consuming, an expense of money and effort for little tangible gain (except for that small percentage of fans who may some day catapult into the ranks of professionals). Furthermore, to an outsider viewing the attendees of an SF convention, it might well appear that to fall among fans is to fall among evil companions.

The first substantial attack on fandom from within the ranks came in the late 1940s, in F. Towner Laney's huge (130 mimeographed pages) and bitter memoir of his life as an SF fan and how fandom had hurt his chances to be normal and successful: "Ah, Sweet Idiocy." Fandom, as described by Laney, is a hotbed of perverts, ineffectuals, and other worthless creatures, vile companions who distract one from the worthwhile pursuits of career and stable human relationships. The attitude is that fandom as a way of life is dangerous to youth and can destroy the proper and normal perspective of an adult upon the priorities of reality. Like the Snark, it will eat you, but not vanish away.

After much fuss, fandom in the early Fifties seems to have granted many of Laney's points and, as a corrective, gotten sillier and more fannish—much less of the open political battling in and among clubs has been reported from that time on, only more personal feuds. But is this better? You don't have to look far into fandom for evidence of childishness and petulance, name-calling, paranoia and nearsightedness. In fact, without the delineation of the substantial influence of fandom on the SF field I have offered, it would be impossible to see anything beyond teenage self-aggrandizing cliques treating each other badly. The legacy of feuds is in reality a legacy of competition for ego gratification, for success on the only terms recognized by fandom ("egoboo").

The world of fandom does not so much reject the values of mundane society as it transmutes them into a system of approval and reward—a replacement for the everyday approval and reward systems that have been unavailable otherwise to the SF writer and the fan until the last few years. As I have shown earlier, until quite recently no SF writer could expect from society either social or literary critical approval for practising his profession, or any substantial money (certainly not enough to equal an average middle-class income). What Laney did not (could not?) recognize is that to enter fandom is to accept its value system as a viable replacement for any other.

Of course such an acceptance can be dangerous to one's normal life in the real world. This is why so many fans leave fandom by the time they are twenty-one. Unarticulated and, perhaps, unexamined, there exists within the heart and soul of every fan a tension between the values of mundane reality and the values of the world of fandom. The best expression of this tension is in the polar-opposite acronyms coined in 1943 and still current: FIJAGH and FIAWOL (see page 163). The population of fandom is drawn from those who are discontented with reality (a quality, as I remarked earlier, of most bright teenagers). The competitive system of fandom may satisfy them, perhaps should satisfy them, only until they are able to succeed in coping with the quotidian world in terms of gaining approval and money in their chosen careers. To the fans, of course, deserters rapidly become nonpersons in the Orwellian sense— the fannish value system must be preserved. Only those fans whose ideals and interests will not permit them to commit themselves wholly to the values of middle-class life, or whose equipment for survival in the middle-class world is poor, remain in fandom.

But while a person remains in fandom and participates in fan activities, the system allows him to rise to whatever level he can and receive his proper share of approval and reward, his name in print in fanzines, whatever. At a time when approval is not forthcoming in everyday life, this can be soul food. Here is a challenging and serious game in which every participant wins, more or less, each according to his deserts.

And the writers win, too. Consider: There is damn little money and critical approval available to a contemporary poet or novelist or short-story writer—perhaps one in a thousand ever even gets a book published, and then the audience is usually only one's peers, normally silent because they too are starving for attention and money. In a system such as this, there are not even table scraps for the SF writer. Except that fandom exists and offers an alternative, the only alternative in the past, and even today, for most SF writers. Until recently, only Ray Bradbury, Robert A. Heinlein, Frank Herbert, Arthur C. Clarke, and Isaac Asimov had outgrown the economic and other boundaries of the SF field and passed beyond the approval or disapproval of fandom into the realms of bestsellerdom. The other possibility now is the legacy of the New Wave—to write works of such transcendent literary quality that critical success outside the SF field is assured (but not money and certainly not the popularity that leads to bestsellerdom). In the long run and for most writers, the approval of fandom is still a safer bet.

Thus, to seek the approval of fandom is of course the most natural thing in the world for a writer or editor who is or was once a fan. And it is a traditional mode for the SF writer, easy to fall into. What is also evident is that fandom may well be substituting one kind of competition for another in the writing community.

It is interesting to examine SF writers in this light. Through wide and long-term contact with the SF writing community, I can testify that some SF writers are openly competitive and some are not, and that there appears to be no direct relationship between fandom and competitiveness. Furthermore, fandom does not generally seem to think of the professionals as competitors vying for their attention and approval but rather as individuals each trying to excel and therefore be worthy. Yet on some level the fans and writers, especially the writers who have emerged from fandom, know that there is just not enough of anything to go around, so these writers go out of their way to attend conventions and win the attention of fandom, and the fan or ex-fan writers who know the ropes and have contacts are certainly best equipped to succeed in this fashion. Perhaps in some cases the personal appeal to fandom may supersede the appeal of the written SF. (This may well have been true with Bob Silverberg in the Fifties and Sixties, until his ambitious works of the late Sixties and early Seventies—his popularity in fandom certainly seems to have been based more on his persona than upon the quality of his writing.) Yet on the whole over the years, SF writers seem to have taken to heart fandom's ideal that each writer should strive to excel in his or her own unique manner and achieve quite individual excellences—you cannot mistake the individual voice of any major SF writer for that of another.

Will the historic relationship between SF and fandom survive the decade of the 1980s? The chances look good at this early date. Certain offshoots of fandom, e.g., *Star Trek* fandom or Amber fandom, may die out, or their fires burn low as did Edgar Rice Burroughs fandom in the 1970s. Or they may split off entirely from SF, as comic book fandom seems to have done. What will keep SF fandom alive is that it seems sure to stay a part of the phenomenon of the SF field, not subordinate to it (as, for instance, football fans are subordinate to football—they are just the customers). Besides, the dominant literary culture in the U.S. and elsewhere does not seem disposed to embrace SF and preempt fandom's role as guardian of the qualities of SF.

Many, though not all, of the chronics and omnivores who make up the wider SF audience are aware of fandom and choose not to become fans. They hear the siren call, perhaps attend a convention or two, but are able to bind themselves to the masts of their daily lives. We have described the SF world earlier as a world which sees itself as being outside the mundane boundaries of contemporary space and time, a world of readers who have attained a new and distanced perspective on the past, present, and future. Well, fandom is the nucleus of the SF world, the center of activity out of which radiate the beams that illuminate the SF world.

Fandom, when examined only as activities, appears to be simply an aggregation of variously eccentric hobbies. But we have seen that it is actually a whole subculture with underlying unities and coherence, of primary significance to an understanding of the SF field.

It's fun, too. Let us not forget that SF is exciting and entertaining escape reading and fandom is similarly an escape from an unrewarding reality into a world of fun and games. The traditions of fandom allow for release of pent-up energies, for outbursts of egregious personal behavior and exhibitionism frowned upon in daily life and, conversely, for normal personal interaction with people whose daily life is bizarre or abnormal in some way (I remember meeting at conventions everything from doctors and attorneys to pornographic filmmakers—and their stars). If you are a professional librarian and feel the desire to walk around wearing a cape, sword, and G-string, go to a convention, where, according to custom, no one will notice unless to compliment you on your originality.

I once accompanied a prominent Boston SF editor new to the field to her first SF convention several years back. At the "meet-the-professionals" cocktail party on Friday evening (which was combined for efficiency with the convention masquerade contest), she expressed some wonder and discomfort at the presence of two attractive women whose costumes consisted of elaborate headdresses and makeup—they were otherwise nude. In a room containing several hundred people, no one seemed to be making a fuss over the two, who walked casually and calmly through the crowd, allowing photographs and accepting admiration. This is not, I explained, a remarkable or uncommon occurrence at a masquerade in SF, although it would certainly not be acceptable at the normal professionals' party. After several years, the editor's jaw is still, I believe, somewhat dropped.

Fun and games, and keeping cool in the face of anyone else's fun and games, are the social rules for convention attendance and for fan activity. I have seen a hundred fans sit and sing till dawn in hotel lobbies, fans in sleeping bags catching naps under tables at parties (day or night), fans wandering in drunken gaggles through motel corridors at 5 A.M. seeking the last open party, fans in deep and serious conversation with a favorite author, fans by the hundreds stripping and jumping in a hotel pool at midnight while members of the convention committee coolly explain to the hotel security officers that this is just a little swimming party and will be supervised. Within very liberal bounds, anything can happen at a science fiction convention—which is part of the fun.

The people you play with are an essential facet of your social life. The sense of community within the SF field, especially among fans and professionals, is founded upon years of the social life of conventions and other fan gatherings, large and small. The fans and professionals eat together, drink together, play together (sleep together, exclude one another, criticize one another), act in some ways as an enormous extended family, complete with poor relations, rebellious children and dimwitted second cousins.

What fandom has done on a social and cultural level for or to the writers in the SF field is to provide them with a paradigm of the life of the writer quite different from the two major paradigms available to all other writers outside SF: the life of the artist (working in isolation from the marketplace to achieve art; supported by the academy, by grants, by awards, perhaps by the admiration of peers) and the life of the commercial writer (after an apprenticeship, writing books and stories or articles primarily for money for big publishers according to the dictates of the marketplace, sometimes actually achieving enough fame to qualify for mention in *People* magazine). Fandom has achieved a redefinition of success and reward for most SF writers.

The life of the SF writer is a life of continual socializing and communication with a rather large audience of loyal and vocal readers together with the majority of other writers working in the field. The response of these people to a writer's work is always in the forefront of his consciousness and may even be the controlling factor in his writing. He feels that he belongs to the same community as all the others, no matter what the personal or professional or aesthetic differences. Most SF writers develop personae in the field identifying them with one of the two mainstream life-style types, but these personae are not (with few exceptions) recognized outside the field and so these writers are actually living the life of SF writers according to the paradigm fandom has established, until or unless they reject the field entirely (as, for instance, Kurt Vonnegut did in the late 1950s). The SF life-style may be the keystone holding the SF field in place and separating it from other genres of contemporary writing.

But the life-style is also restrictive and not to the taste of some writers. Many SF writers, including John D. MacDonald, Richard McKenna, and Donald E. Westlake, have abandoned SF entirely in favor of the success of the commercial writer. (No one I know has yet abandoned SF to live the artist's life, since you can have all the disadvantages of an artist's life and still remain an SF writer—although perhaps one might say that a majority of the New Wave writers of the Sixties did in fact attempt the life of the artist seriously for a time.)

Fandom, then, is at the center of a discussion of SF, without which all else flies apart. Fandom is what makes for SF a world of difference.

IV THE FUTURE OF SF

11 "Let's Get SF Back in the Gutter Where It Belongs"

LITERARY critics have a private language that they have developed over the last century, a large and precise technical vocabulary that allows them to communicate with each other quickly and efficiently, just like the medical shorthand surgeons use in the operating room or the specialized diction of philosophers. This private language is opaque to outsiders; in fact, it excludes everyone but insiders.

The leading theoretical critic in the science fiction field for over ten years, Professor Darko Suvin of Montreal's McGill University, has been producing a series of papers on science fiction remarkable for their innovative critical insights and for their total lack of communication to any but a small group of advanced critics in and outside the SF field. Therefore Suvin's name is anathema to almost everyone in the SF field, all of whom have totally missed the point: that Suvin is attempting to analyze and describe what exists—using accepted technical vocabulary—not merely expressing his sentiments on the value of SF. The value is implied by the serious nature of the discussion, though his work is only of the most tangential relevance to the field as is being written today, for criticism can deal only with what has happened.

Alarms reverberate throughout the fanzines and echo through the halls of convention hotels. "SF will be destroyed if writers take critics seriously and begin to write for an audience of teachers and article-writers, the academics who rule fashionable taste in the Western world!" This is all too true. All critics, even the best, must set up paradigms based on past literature in order to proceed to analyze a new work. Since a new work is never an utterly precise imitation of a paradigm (see Borges's wonderful fiction, "Pierre Menard, Author of 'Don Quixote' "), all new works are criticized, held up to examination against the ideal pattern, and found wanting.

The demonic paradox is that SF has always attempted to deal with change and the future, to establish new paradigms, and so has been found not just unsuccessful according to the accepted paradigms of contemporary literature (Joyce, Lawrence, Bellow, Mailer, Heller, etc.), but also completely unfashionable and therefore totally beyond the pale, unacceptable reading material for all properly educated people.

And so bad critics (by far the majority of all critics), especially fashionable and popular critics whose reputations depend on defending a conservative value system based on the paradigms of the past, have lambasted science fiction consistently for decades, giving most of the serious writers in the field a serious case of paranoia, mostly justified by the facts.

What to do? The unfavorable criticism of SF by academics and fashionable critics, who really are arbiters of taste in our society, has wounded many fine artists and writers in SF for years, to the point where some have denied writing SF at all (such as Kurt Vonnegut and Harlan Ellison, for a time) and others have accepted the critically imposed doublethink, usually phrased "This work is so good, so well-crafted, poignant and powerful that it is not really SF, it just seems to be on the surface" (examples are Ray Bradbury's *The Martian Chronicles* and Daniel Keyes's *Flowers for Algernon*). The final proof, to fashionable critics, that SF is somehow by definition (note the irony) bad art is that the writers make money writing—oh, not a hell of a lot of money, but they care about it and are therefore tainted by commercialism. Real artists, one supposes, must be independently wealthy, have royal patrons, or starve nobly while writing on butcher's paper. Then, too, SF writers are accused of lack of realism.

It's actually the theoreticians such as Darko Suvin and Robert Scholes and Joanna Russ who are doing the real work of criticism—which most of the practical critics who form popular taste (after all, they write entertaining essays with clever and sharp put-downs) haven't read because it wasn't taught at Princeton back when they were there and besides they have not much better an understanding of the technical language of theoretical criticism than the rest of us. Reading a technical paper in any field, after all, is hard work and doesn't score you any more points when you are writing a "critical" review for *Time* or *Newsweek,* whose audience doesn't want accepted taste challenged anyway.

So, as it has happened, the talented amateur critics in the SF fanzines, and the writer/critics (such as James Blish, Damon Knight, and Algis Budrys), and the vocal fans who approach authors at conventions and express subjective critical reactions to SF works, have all, as a group, formed the critical audience for SF and kept the authors and the field alive and growing since the 1930s. The SF field has created its own imprecise critical terminology ("It works/it doesn't work") which, until the new theoreticians of the Seventies and their beginnings at synthesizing SF and "mundane" critical concepts, has been a more effective and accurate tool for surveying the science fictional landscape than any other because it takes the essential aims and foci of SF into account—especially the notion, thoroughly understood by all authors and devotees of SF, that within the confines of a respect for realism given an imagined world, innovation is a key virtue. Cordwainer Smith and Larry Niven, for instance, are writers revered in the field for their innovation, for new and colorful changes rung on standard SF situations.

But just at the moment when the first stirrings of incorporation and adaptation of traditional criticism appeared on the SF scene, in the late 1960s, a large number of the most literate and advanced SF authors and readers misunderstood the signal flags and misinterpreted the new levels of criticism as either unprovoked attacks on SF (an attempt to criticize it and them out of existence) or as a prescription for the SF of the future. Yes, after decades of paranoia and disrepute, the big guns of literary criticism were going to pay attention (ah, respectability!), and the avant-garde (for which read "the new wave to which I belong") will triumph in popularity—as long as I can behave in a manner proper to literary lions. For which read: as long as what I write has enough of the literary virtues which these top honchos are comfortable with and can praise.

There was much less that was new and colorful in science fiction in the 1970s and early 1980s, given the enormous amount published, than in any previous decade. The recent past in SF has been a time of consolidation and wide public acceptance. But the new wider audience is unfamiliar with the peculiar innovative virtues of SF; both this audience and the reviewers, for the most part, have encouraged more psychological depth in characterization, less technical and scientific vocabulary and near-future settings, to which a wide audience can relate without uncomfortable demands on the willing suspension of disbelief. If this trend continues, success really could spoil science fiction.

Already the field is showing signs of enthusiastic capitulation to a level of popular taste outside the boundaries of the genre audiences. After all, writers want to be liked, preferably by everyone, and, as we noticed earlier, SF writers are used to being paid for their work—not much, in the past, but with the enormous growth in popularity and respectability for written SF in the 1970s, the top writers in the field in the 1980s are in demand and are suddenly commanding prices for their works approaching or in the six-figure range. And in the recent past it has become possible for almost any novice out of school to sell an SF novel for a few thousand dollars. This is particularly significant in an era when a young writer in any other field must struggle for years to get a first novel published (and most often gives up after several years of rejection). SF is a wide open and expanding market amenable to partial successes.

But the cost of these enormous rewards (money, wide popularity, critical praise) is already showing in several ways. A number of young, talented writers who have read some SF have written one or several novels in the field and then stepped out of it as quickly as possible into even more commercial areas, having established publishing contacts and contributed competent rehashes of SF clichés to the body of written SF. Other writers have entered SF without particular knowledge of it or regard for it because they make money there. They stay in the field but do everything possible to avoid the creative enterprise of SF, substituting creative vocabulary for innovation (James Blish once wrote a scathing denunciation of this approach to SF which he called "naming rabbits as smeerps"—they remain rabbits in spite of being cute little hopping furry smeerps). A lot of them write mostly fantasy. Most unsettling of all to lovers of SF, some of the major writers have been seduced by prosperity into expanding the scope of their SF novels to include large casts of engaging minor characters, panoramic disasters, obligatory sex romantically described, vast superficial detail, all the elements of the fat best-seller novel: Gregory Benford and William Rotsler's *Shiva Descending* (1979) and Larry Niven and Jerry Pournelle's *Lucifer's Hammer* (1977) are examples. In addition, some writers have expanded their popular works into series, especially trilogies, but also four, five, or more volumes: Frank Herbert's *Dune* trilogy is now stretched to five volumes, all best-sellers.

Who is to say that any of these people are wrong in their personal choices, but the end result is certainly a dilution of the SF enterprise (somewhat parallel to the dilution of atmosphere at very large conventions)—not the attitude that has prevailed in the field since the Twenties, which has been its great strength. Enormous pressures from the marketplace have limited SF's freedom to create new visions.

Not that any writer paid for writing is ever entirely free of the demands of the market—there have been restrictions, sometimes severe, on sex in SF, on pessimistic SF, on all sorts of things dictated by various markets. But with truly big-time commercial success, for the first time since the category developed there is pressure on all sides to downplay the former center of attention and appeal—the science fictional content—in favor of stylistic virtues, characterization, complex panoramic story, near-future setting, all of which will broaden the market for a work in this wider field and will insure more favorable critical and review response from outsiders.

The fans have changed too. A local (as opposed to national) SF convention in 1970 and for years before that would be attended by anywhere from thirty to fifty to at most 350 fans and writers. Local conventions were held in nearly twenty areas in the U.S. and sporadically elsewhere. In 1979, there were five local conventions held on the same Memorial Day weekend in different parts of the U.S., all with attendances of from 400 to 1,000 fans. Obviously fandom has expanded enormously and often chaotically in the last decade. But the change is more than numerical expansion. Prior to 1970, you could make the reliable assumption that any fan, every fan, had read or should read most of the famous authors and works of science fiction, if only in order to discuss in an informed way which ones are classics.

The assumption of knowledge of SF writings has been glue holding the whole thing together for decades, really since the very beginnings in the late 1920s. Suddenly in the early 1970s, however, the SF world began to change. A large number, then a larger number, of the people living in this world were neophytes, teenagers exposed to the SF world without being addicted to the written works. The success of *Star Trek, 2001, Stranger in a Strange Land* and *Dune,* Marvel Comics and the whole comics convention movement (an outgrowth, like the *Star Trek* conventions, of SF fans launching analogous conventions) all contributed much more than the magazines and the books to a sudden and profound increase in the number of fans, especially the number of fans attending conventions. And most of these new fans found the SF world through popular culture (one or more of the aforementioned pop classics), not from the omnivorous reading that characterized all earlier fans. Some of them became overnight omnivores, but many of them, perhaps most, never delved into large numbers of the stories and novels of the past.

They came too late, you see. Even by 1971, with ninety or so new SF books being published by the industry in that year, it was nearly impossible to read all the new stuff, let alone catch up on the old. At a recent convention, in a room containing nearly twenty young fans, a discussion was in progress about the early works of J. G. Ballard, works that had sent shock waves of admiration and enthusiasm (and, as I observed earlier, debate) throughout the field in the late Fifties and early Sixties. Only one of the twenty had read any Ballard. At the Clarion SF writers workshop in 1971, in a roomful of aspiring SF writers *all* of whom have since published stories and novels, only one of eighteen had ever read a novel by Philip K. Dick, surely one of the great SF masters of the last three decades. By 1984, the written SF field is no longer knowable in its entirety to the average fan or the average young author.

Yes, the same social conditions obtain in fandom as I have discussed, but the vision of what SF is and what it can do in fandom has changed. The written word is still the primary influence, establishes the primary image of what SF is and what its possibilities might be. But the younger writers and the younger fans got their initial imprint of SF from sci-fi, from media. No wonder the field is in a state of change and confusion as it escalates in the Eighties. Success, growth, will certainly change SF. It already has.

The decade of the Seventies was the greatest boom period in the contemporary history of SF. More people, writers, fans, and publishers entered the field than ever before. But a whole lot of that boom was illusory. You see, it wasn't all that much a science fiction boom. A lot of the success of SF in the Seventies wasn't at the center of the field but around the edges—particularly in the field of fantasy (handled by science fiction editors and publishers, written by science fiction writers and read by science fiction fans, but not SF). The success of fantasy tended to obscure the real fact that not that much more actual SF was being written and published than in the Sixties, not a boom decade. A huge amount, in some months more than 50 percent, of the SF of the Seventies was actually reprinted from earlier decades. The paperback industry is like that, always trying to capitalize on the fact that SF doesn't date like most other fiction. Whenever an author is hot because of a good new book, all his previous books from years back return to print. If the figures are examined closely, less than 100 new SF books appeared in any year of the 1970s—after you exclude all the fantasy. And the SF magazines dropped steadily in circulation over the decade. A strange boom.

SF, in the 1970s and today, is a capacious umbrella for a multitude of hybrid forms of fantasy, surrealism, weird tales, and pop retreads of all SF ideas. Another breakdown in definition is happening. Perhaps we need sympathetic, knowledgeable criticism, theoretical criticism, now more than ever to keep track of where we are. Certainly we need literary history for the first time, so that we do not forget where we have been.

Do we need an academy of science fiction arts? No, because the essence of the field is change and we do not need to be frozen in place. But maybe we need the boom to bust, so that SF may remain knowable at all and not disappear into the agglomeration of contemporary literature, thereby losing its capacity for innovation, some of which is gained only by its juxtaposition to current literary fashion.

This juxtaposition, though, needs some further elucidation. Only a minority of the educated population of the Western world knows much or cares much about literary fashion. SF is not now and never has been fashionable among those who do care. It is and has been fashionable for decades among scientists and engineers, for whom early SF was an amusing diversion, a spur to speculation, and an inspiration for the future—a literature that took them and their real work into account even when it did not place them at the center of everything important happening in Western civilization. Most scientists and engineers do not read SF in adult life, but many of them did at some point—many of them were early omnivores. At a cocktail party of members of the physics department from your local university, you will not find many department members or students who will deny ever having read SF, whereas at an English department party you will be hard pressed to find any present or former readers. You will probably even find, among the physics types, one or more individuals who has a friend who is a fan, or who knows an SF writer, or who has even tried to write it himself. As long as there remains a "two cultures" split in society (as noted by C. P. Snow), the other culture will need its nonliterary literature, SF, into which their ideas feed and feed back. For fun. And as a bridge between science and literature.

Literary fashion, to those who care about it and guard it, is the Great Game of each era. Consider: It is the Elizabethan age and you wish to be a writer. You must of course be a poet and display your mastery of literary art through the sonnet form. There are certainly other poetic forms through which you can woo fame—the varieties of lyric, pastoral, epic—but the Great Game is the sonnet. If you write something such as drama, crass and popular, you can't even publish it as part of your "works" without being ridiculed. Back to the present: Fashion dictates that you play the game of Hemingway/Faulkner/Bellow/Barth if you are a novelist (or the bigger game of Mann, Joyce, Lawrence, Nabokov, Camus) in order to be admitted to the literary playing field. SF today is still to Literature as drama was to the sonnet in the age of Shakespeare, to a large extent bad art and in the opinion of many insiders who reject literary fashion, such as del Rey, not art at all, just craftwork and fun.

That's why a young electronics engineer, for instance, who has had just enough literary education by way of required courses to know that literature is the highly protected preserve of experts (not something you can have an opinion on, such as religion or politics), can start writing SF in her spare time, submit it for publication, and expect it to reach an open and uncritical, in the college lit. course sense, audience if it is published. SF is apart from the literary game, so that any enthusiast is welcome to play—especially anyone with a scientific background of any sort who might introduce new ideas into the common repository of the SF field.

If you play the Great Game of literary art in your era, you may not make a false move or you are dead, because all your competition is making the same moves at the same time, and all but a very few must fall short of true excellence. (We can't, after all, waste time reading the top two hundred Elizabethan sonneteers—we just read the top five or ten—and so with novelists.) Somehow you know that you are by definition an outsider to the Great Game when you set out to write and read SF. As we have seen, this can be enormously liberating to writer and reader.

But the threat of Literature and the mandarin culture of art is always present to seduce writer and reader away from SF. Oh, sigh, the large majority of twelve-year-olds who have their sentience first awakened by SF pass beyond it into the empyrean realms of fashionable taste—some would call it normalcy. And do not mistake their gains: They become serious and well adjusted, sometimes they even become responsible adults, an attainment of no small worth in the world of the future. But they rarely pass into the world of literary fashion, because the whole mind-set of SF discourages such a transitory game, with such likelihood of failure.

At least until recently. In the last decade or so, SF has become the only game in town for many young writers, including a bunch with knowledge of fashion and literary taste, some even with advanced writing degrees(!). They all know that fashion is a snob and they wish to be part of the few, the elite. Some play the Great Game.

The best of them whom the field honors, for instance Joanna Russ and Thomas M. Disch, really do manage to accomplish art and SF at the same time. But the rest *use* SF as a back entrance to the fields of literature. And while they may produce works of some merit to people of taste, they are becoming dangerous to the SF field just because there are so many of them, and they write so well, and they get published and praised by peers—but they aren't really contributing to the SF field. Rather, they are often taking something from it by creating a major distraction, a confusion of goals. This is one pernicious legacy of the New Wave for fans.

Dena Benatan, a young fan in the early 1970s, was one of the first to notice the post-New Wave dangers presented to the field by the new and intense interest in SF by academics and outside critics, who for the most part concentrated their attention on the younger fringes of the SF writing community, just these new young artists I have been discussing. With typical fannish humor, she coined the phrase, "Let's get Science Fiction back in the gutter where it belongs," and popularized it as the rallying cry of SF people who do not want their field preempted and used by outsiders without sincere contributions and due respect.

Benatan's slogan is not to be confused with the not entirely coincidental movement popularized by Lester del Rey in the early 1970s, which we mentioned earlier, to paraphrase: "Let's get back to roots, to good old-fashioned science fiction that is *pure entertainment*. No more aspiration to art—the 'New Wave' has ebbed." Benatan and del Rey both responded to a complex of changes in the early 1970s evident to the whole field, but generally unarticulated. For the first time the SF field was large, relatively prosperous, respectable to outsiders for a variety of reasons, and even well-written in many cases (more often than ever before). Given all this, why was almost everyone in the field disturbed—why wasn't it as much fun any more?

Back in the 1950s, when the tenets of contemporary taste in SF were established in the field, the sin of "little-magazine-fiction-dressed-up-as-SF" was acknowledged as one of the deadlies right up there along with "hackwork" and "western-dressed-up-as-SF" (space opera). Damon Knight, Anthony Boucher, James Blish, Judith Merril, Theodore Sturgeon—the SF critical establishment of the 1950s—stood firmly behind the principle that SF could and should aspire to art; but of course it should stay SF while doing so.

By the late 1960s, as we have seen, Merril and others had changed position to the extent that SF that aspires to art is spec fic, and transcends the mere genre of SF (sound of warning bells, alarms, sirens, danger flags—genre about to be obliterated!). A reactionary decade ensued, during which the "SF is entertainment" dictum of del Rey, Spider Robinson, and Donald A. Wollheim (no matter how dunderheaded its expression on some occasions) seriously helped to keep the field viable as a commercial category of publishing, while Tom Disch, Joanna Russ, Samuel R. Delany, Ursula K. Le Guin, and a few others aspired to art. Algis Budrys, who maintained the clearest vision of SF and art throughout the decade, wrote too little criticism to create a major countervailing force (equivalent to the Knight/ Blish/Merril axis of the 50s). And academic criticism of the field remained too often (always excepting the theoreticians and historians) irrelevant and rather naïve. The battle to keep SF in the gutter was joined.

From the outside, it is often hard to discern what has been going on. Leslie Fiedler, in his most recent comments on SF (in

What Was Literature?, New York: Simon & Schuster, 1982, pp. 121–22), characterizes the proceedings somewhat patronizingly: "Only in the United States has there ever been a long-lived venture into non-elitist criticism, and that uniquely American [Fiedler seems unaware of the active participation of British fans] experiment would, it seems to me, repay close examination both in terms of how it succeeded and how it failed. I am referring to the 'fanzines.' " He goes on to present the fans as an "impassioned, cohesive and exclusivist audience, whose taste was defined by both a preference for a particular literary kind of fiction and a rejection of almost everything else, from the mimetic best sellers their parents read to the 'classics' their teachers assigned." It should be evident that something larger than Fiedler perceived has been happening.

The battle for higher standards is real, but all the names have been changed to keep outsiders from finding out what the real issues are and have been. Insiders use slogans, ironies, arcane references, confusions in this war. Because the tangible rewards changed in the 1970s—more money, public acceptance (academic and social), the real rewards of the mundane world which confer power upon the SF community—this war was more meaningful than the continuing battle over names and definitions. The war to get SF back into the gutter is a real war for the minds and hearts of the SF community, and the final battles have not yet been won or lost.

What happened? Well, the 1970s was a decade of more wordage and less innovation in the field than in ever before. The best 10 percent of SF was as good or better than any previous decade, especially better written as a rule according to the standards of outsiders (Le Guin, Disch, Moorcock, Russ, Budrys, et al.). But the younger, newer writers (with such honorable exceptions as James Tiptree, Jr., John Varley, Vonda McIntyre) started with less knowledge of the repository of SF ideas and less concern for the core, in-field audience's tastes and preferences than ever before (and not, like the "New Wavicles" of the 1960s, knowing it all and rejecting it as a revolutionary act). In addition, the much larger audiences of the 1970s and early 1980s were less knowledgeable and less demanding, less familiar with the classics. The field began to lose its coherence through sheer size and diffusion. The most popular and success-ful books of the decade were film novelizations and continu-ations of series (*Star Wars, Star Trek* books, *Children of Dune,* etc.), all of which outsold by miles, for instance, the winners of the Hugo and Nebula awards of the decade. The SF best-sellers, such as Herbert's *Children of Dune* or Heinlein's *The Number of the Beast,* rarely won the awards for excellence in the field, were hardly ever even nominated. What a change from earlier times!

The 1970s was also the decade of fantasy's great success in the marketplace. As we noted earlier, with the phenomenal and enduring popularity of the Tolkien books in the late 1960s and the strong resurgence of popularity of Robert E. Howard's barbarian hero, Conan, at the same time, fantasy in paperback began to appear with some regularity in the late 1960s and with increasing frequency in the 1970s.

Both of these types of fantasy—the amoral/heroic and the moral/chivalric—were and are published as parts of SF pub-lishing programs by various houses. They take up budgets and schedule space that would otherwise be devoted to SF. In addition, supernatural horror fantasy burst into best-seller prominence noticeably and often during the decade. Although the authors of these best-sellers were sometimes graduates of the SF field, such as Stephen King, the field did not acknowledge their relationship to SF until the founding of the World Fantasy Convention in 1975. Ironically this convention began, over the following years, to accelerate a unification of the various types of fantasy into a self-conscious unit analogous to but separate from the SF field (with many crossover practitioners, writers and readers). There is a huge and loyal mass audience for fantasy at the present time, but an audience of what C. S. Lewis would have called bad readers: those almost wholly uncritical and seemingly ready to reward the most repetitive and gory spectacles—and very powerful because of vast numbers in the mass audience outside the field.

Whether the incipient self-conscious split between fantasy and SF will continue is a large question for the 1980s. Certain estimates of the expansion of the SF field in the 1970s depended upon including large numbers of fantasy books, as I have noted earlier. If it turns out that the fantasy boom really masked a steady state for the SF field during most of the 1970s, then a crisis of self-consciousness will hit the SF field which could be fruitful and productive. Or it could mean just another bust in the market.

If, on the other hand, the SF and fantasy fields remain intimately linked and the popular success of fantasy stays high or increases, less and less new SF will actually be published for lack of room in publishing schedules, truly a disaster for SF. The SF field has never been larger, in all ways, than it is right now in the 1980s, but both doom-and-bust and popularity-and-expansion may be just around the corner, in some complex conjunction.

Oh, nostalgia for the gutter—are fans really alienated or did they just use to be? Will success finally destroy SF, when it has kept the faith through so much adversity?

The 1970s was a decade of fatigue and retrenchment and disillusionment in our culture, no new energy sources and an exhaustion of the old ones, literally or figuratively. A twelve-year-old can no longer enter the SF field and become an influential, world-famous Big Name Fan by the age of eighteen—the field is too large now, the numbers too large. One Hugo-winning fanzine in the 1960s printed only 100 copies—in the 1970s, no fanzine with a circulation less than 1,000 won the Hugo, and then, in nine out of ten years, the winner's circulation was 1,500 to 4,000 (the "semipros" took over). Fandom is dominated by fans over thirty and there are now so many of them, after generations of fandom have passed, that there is not only no room at the top but the top is damn difficult to locate until you have been a fan for a while. Thousands of fanzines circulate every year, thousands of titles! This is a new kind of adversity for the field—diffusion, loss of traditional focus.

Remember that Judith Merril and her friends in the Fifties never expected the SF field to grow much larger, certainly not as large as it is now. After all, you can't have an alienated, advanced, elite majority, now can you? Yet as SF grows and its influence on our culture increases, it begins to seem less alienated, less advanced, less elite, a majority phenomenon. Back into the gutter means away from the elitism of high art and literary culture, but not toward the mass popularity of *Rosemary's Baby* and *Battlestar Galactica* (fantasy and sci-fi, respectively). Back to the gutter means back to the socially unacceptable, to the real edges of our culture, the primal energies of the play of crazy ideas, the core of wonder, to the testing of realities and the joy of prophetic vision, to the revolutionary fervor of the Futurian Society, of Campbell the editor, of Boucher and Gold, Blish and Knight, Moorcock and Merril, Harlan Ellison and J. J. Pierce.

Science fiction has been moving upward over the years from the underground, the unfashionable world, the gutter, toward the world of fashion. As the field has grown and prospered, it has continually felt the pressures of the opposing forces of art and money drawing SF writers away from the in-field audience, either toward best-seller writing forms or the various pop culture media (both being special cases of sci-fi), or toward the Great Game of fashionable literature or counterfashion of the literary avant-garde (both being special cases of the pull toward speculative fiction).

The SF field has to resist the forces of money from commercial success outside the field, and the forces of aesthetic success according to outside standards, rules that deny the validity of the SF enterprise in and of itself. In the gutter, the pull of these forces is more elemental and therefore easier to recognize and combat—you know damn well that you are betraying the ideals of the SF field if you support or create sci-fi or that you are denying the existence of valid literary ideals in the SF field by attempting to conform to any set of avant-garde or experimental literary principles—and the rewards are generally smaller (less money on the one hand, less fame and recognition on the other—and no respectability in either case, right where you started). The very large amounts of money and respectability which the fashionable world offers that draws writers away from the SF field are beguiling in the extreme, the rewards any other writer of any kind would cherish. Under such pressure, the SF field must surely be sundered and dispersed unless it maintains a conscious independence.

"Let's get SF back into the gutter where it belongs" is the rallying cry of those in SF who are most conscious of the need for independence, for the clarity of vision that will allow the field to endure the tension between art and money without fleeing its own center of being, diluting or rejecting its own traditional virtues. It will remain the greatest test of the inner culture of the SF world, of fandom, that it must reward the best writers in the field enough and convincingly enough to keep each of them from fleeing, from aspiring to virtues other than those we have examined in previous chapters as characteristic of SF, and from emigrating to the world of fashionable literature either for profit from or the respect of "the Establishment."

And indeed after a decade of argument now, at least the issues are becoming clearer than, for instance, during the New Wave battles of the latter 1960s. The SF field has arrived in the future and must now question the value of its own ideas of progress. The works of such authors as Gene Wolfe, Michael Bishop, and Gregory Benford (to mention the three most recent winners of the Science Fiction Writers of America Nebula Award for best novel of the year) are accomplished and respectable contributions to the contemporary American novel, yet still in the field. The most serious reassessment of science fiction and the achievement of its writers is still to come.

12 Crawling Home from the Future

THE world of science fiction is only one of the subworlds that contribute to our contemporary culture, from the sublime to the perverse. The effort I have expended to illuminate and clarify this particular underground and its activities has been meant to show how thoroughly the science fiction world has established itself as a significant influence upon what we may as well call the dominant culture of Western civilization.

It is in the nature of dominant cultures to assure their continued dominance by ignoring the existence of competing cultures for as long as possible or, when it is no longer possible, to attack those cultures as bad/worthless and, at the extreme limit, to integrate said culture into the dominant culture and then deny it ever existed outside. The world of SF was ignored for decades and then, as we have shown, attacked as worthless for more decades. We are now in a period of transition between attack and attempted absorption, and in a period of vigorous growth within the SF world. It is not for us to say that the attempts now being made (and for the last ten to fifteen years) will not succeed in the near future. Yet considering the rather high degree of success the SF world has had thus far in the twentieth century in retaining its independence (it has already outlasted the "Beatnik" culture, which it preceded, for instance), the influence of SF is not about to abate, even though many of the images of SF are diluted or altered as they pass into general usage in our mass culture. (For example, an android, in SF, is a human simulacrum, distinct from a robot—a distinction destroyed by the "droid" R2D2 in *Star Wars*.)

Through examining various aspects of SF and the SF world from a general perspective, I have tried to present a portrait of the science fiction world accessible to outsiders: its history and development, its inner struggles, the face it exposes to the public. This guided tour and maps of the terrain, the description and analysis of how the elements of the SF world are related and function in place, of how SF literature relates to the culture from which it emerges, are intended to resolve into a whole the counterculture or alternate reality: the SF field, a positive alternative to the dominant culture of our world.

You have seen how the activities of the fans and the efforts of the professionals to create works for and within the field have resulted in a uniquely powerful and independent force running separate from the mainstream for fifty years but constantly flowing into it and altering its color and consistency. As stated at the outset of this book, I am not in the business of winning converts to SF. If you wish to extend your knowledge of the field by reading further in the literature, well and good. But my major thrust has been to draw attention to the fact that not only the literature but the whole SF world is *there*, that it exists, that its existence should be taken into account. And that this consistent and evolving world depicted and toured is neither without worth nor is necessarily evil—just, certainly, different.

What next?

Science fiction is a literature and state of mind that expresses a certain edge in human history, in the evolution of Western civilization. That edge is the crest of the wave of human knowledge and power over the material world, of the belief that knowledge is power which is the driving force of technological civilization. A hallmark of SF is the attitude, "What will we do about the future, how will we make it?" Science fiction presupposes human authority in and over the physical universe. It is in no way an appropriate response to the coming inhospitable reality of "what will happen no matter what we do." It is not a literature of acceptance.

In the next decades we may expect to see science fiction reach even greater heights of popular acceptance and influence, for it is the characteristic literature of our time. But as "our time" gives way to a truly new era we can expect to see SF vanish into the history of literature. Something tells us that the people of the future will not be as impressed with the notion of the future as we are.

For more than fifty years now, the SF field has been with us, growing in strength, breadth, and influence until it colors our whole perception of the contemporary world. Yet it is persistently seen by the world at large as a fad that mushroomed out of nowhere just the other day—as though it all started with *Star Wars*—and that will no doubt vanish into dust next season or the season after that. The bloom fades from the spaceship fast in our world of enthusiasms and revolutions in public tastes. But get set for a lot more SF, because our world is still changing fast and SF is the only literature that is well prepared to respond to change.

Indeed, we may be sure that science fiction as a separate and distinguishable field will become indistinguishable from Literature with the demise of the temporary phenomenon that spawned it: the technological revolution of the twentieth century. However, that wave of power still drives our civilization and has not yet broken. Science fiction still illuminates our group consciousness to an extent only partially recognized.

In the everyday world, many artists and writers totally unrelated to the science fiction field are expressing their vision partly or wholly in images from SF, sometimes powerfully, sometimes awkwardly—architects, automobile designers, and advertising executives all use images and ideas whose ultimate source is the SF world. We are living, as I stated earlier, in yesterday's SF future. And tomorrow will be more like science fiction than ever, like it or not. This is not a statement of advocacy but an observation of fact.

The vision of the future, the idea of a future world as a "place" at a traceable and definable distance from this point in time, the present, with certain general association clusters (things are worse versus things are better) is almost wholly an invention of the SF field, as is the idea that through extrapolation we may apply selected causes in the present to obtain certain effects in the future, and of course the idea that the future world is very different from the present. SF literature is prophetic; it may even be predictive in very specific ways.

The fans and writers in the SF field have known these facts and taken these ideas into account since the 1930s. Some of the greatest arguments in fandom in the early days were over what the people in SF could do about their perceptions of the future, especially whether there were actions in the real world to be taken to influence the future directly. Each fan and writer has responded individually to this challenge in daily life, but the SF field as a whole has consistently rejected any group actions outside the SF world (remember the amusing story of Claude Degler and his Cosmic Circle) in favor of the primary activity of the SF field: to support through fan or professional activities the creation of more and better science fiction. Outsiders may *use* SF or SF images and ideas of the future, but within the world of SF, the vision of the future is its own justification, its own reward.

Meanwhile, many readers have found in SF a literature filled with useful ideas that may be applied to the conduct of life in the world today: to invent, to predict, to insulate oneself against the waves of scientific and technological change that sweep continuously across the sands of the twentieth century. It does no harm to the SF world to use its literature for your own purposes. I submit, however, that you do the SF world an injustice and yourself intellectual harm if you pervert the idea of the *use* of SF into seeing it as a medium with a *purpose*.

What do I predict? In the media, sci-fi will continue to be profitable and popular throughout at least the next decade. Already multitudes of projects are in the works to capitalize on the successes of the last decade. (*Star Wars* has been the single most profitable film of all time to date; *Star Trek*, a failed TV show of the Sixties, turned into one of the most phenomenally successful properties of the Seventies and Eighties, whose fans were able to influence the president of the U.S. to name the first space shuttle the *Enterprise*.) You are going to be seeing a whole lot more sci-fi. And if we may extrapolate from the past, the consistent presentation of science fictional images will project these images into our cultural consciousness and continue to influence our perceptions of reality.

The essential response of the SF field has been to create more and better SF. Keep it light, keep it entertaining, keep it changing—the only escape is into visions of possibilities as yet unimagined, of what we will do about it when the time comes. Some SF stories predict solutions. Others warn, "This is what it will be like unless something is done now." But most stories continue to play visionary games, and this is the mainstream of the SF field.

Science fiction is criticism of reality. More and better-written SF is being written and published now than ever before. The community is vigorous, active, larger than ever before.

The golden age of science fiction is the present.

INDEX